# The Newest
## 30-Day Whole Food
### Cookbook for Beginners

30-Day Whole Food Recipes to Help You Start a New
Way of Eating with a 30 Days Diet Plan

**Claudia Hendrix**

# CONTENT

If you're looking to start eating healthier, one of the best places to start is by incorporating more whole foods into your diet. And what better way to do that than with a cookbook specifically devoted to whole foods recipes? The 30-Day Whole Foods Cookbook is a great resource for anyone wanting to transition to a healthier way of eating. The book is divided into four weeks, with each week featuring recipes that focus on a different type of whole food. Week one focuses on fruits and vegetables, week two features whole grains, week three spotlights protein-rich foods, and week four highlights healthy fats. In addition to recipes, the book also includes tips on how to shop for and prepare whole foods and information on the health benefits of each type of food. Whether you're a complete novice in the kitchen or a seasoned pro, the 30-Day Whole Foods Cookbook has something for everyone. Make sure you have plenty of whole foods on hand so you don't get tempted to cheat. Batch cooking will help you save time and stay on track. This challenge is all about eating whole foods for 30 days. That means eating foods that are unprocessed and unrefined. This includes fruits, vegetables, whole grains, nuts, and seeds. The challenge may seem daunting at first, but it's not as difficult as it sounds. Start by slowly incorporating more whole foods into your diet. And be sure to plan so you have healthy meals and snacks on hand. With a little effort, you can easily stick to the challenge and reap the benefits of eating whole foods.

## What Is 30-Day Whole Foods?

Are you looking to jumpstart your healthy eating habits? Why not try a 30-Day Whole Foods challenge? Eating whole foods is a great way to improve your health and energy levels. It can also help you lose weight and feel better overall. If you want to improve your diet and eat more whole foods, you may consider a 30-Day Whole Foods challenge. This type of challenge requires you to eat only whole foods for 30 days and typically eliminates processed foods, added sugars, and refined grains from your diet. Whole foods are generally considered to be healthier than processed foods, as they're minimally processed and often contain more vitamins, minerals, and fiber. Eating a diet rich in whole foods has been linked with various health benefits, including a lower risk of chronic diseases such as heart disease, diabetes, and cancer. If you're thinking of undertaking a 30-Day Whole Foods challenge, it's important to plan and make sure you have enough whole foods on hand. You'll also want to make sure you're getting enough variety in your diet, as eating the same foods every day can quickly become monotonous. If you're looking to improve your eating habits and cut out processed foods, you may be considering a 30-Day Whole Foods challenge. The 30-Day Whole Foods is a month-long program that asks participants to eat only whole, unprocessed foods. This means no processed meats, grains, dairy,

legumes, alcohol, or added sugars. The challenge is meant to help you reset eating habits and break any reliance on unhealthy, processed foods. If you're thinking of embarking on a 30-Day Whole Foods challenge, there are a few things you should know. First, the challenge is not for the faint of heart. It's a major change from the Standard American Diet, and it can be tough to stick to at first. However, many people find that the challenge is well worth it, as it can lead to improved energy levels, better sleep, and increased focus. To succeed on the 30-Day Whole Foods, you'll need to be prepared. This means stocking your kitchen with whole, unprocessed foods.

## 30-Day Whole Food Challenges

The challenge is simple: for 30 days, eat whole foods. That means unprocessed, unrefined, and straight from nature. No artificial flavors, colors, or preservatives. The goal is to improve your overall health, energy levels, and quality of sleep.  The first step is to assess your current diet. Track everything you eat and drink for 3 days, including water. Be as specific as possible, including portion sizes. This will give you a baseline to measure your progress. Then, it's time to clean out your pantry and fridge. Toss anything that doesn't fit the challenge criteria. This may seem drastic, but starting with a clean slate is important. Are you up for a challenge? If you're interested in eating healthier, then you may want to try the 30-Day Whole Foods challenge. This means eating ONLY whole foods for 30 days - no processed foods, no artificial ingredients, and no junk food. It may sound daunting, but it can be done! Here are a few tips to help you succeed. Plan ahead. This is key to any successful challenge. Decide what meals you're going to eat and make a grocery list accordingly. Prep meals in advance. This will help you stay on track when you're feeling hungry and don't have time to cook. Find a friend or family member to do the challenge with you. Having someone to support you will make it much easier. Allow yourself some flexibility. If you slip up and eat something that isn't allowed, don't beat yourself up. Just get back on track the next day. If you're considering taking on the

30-Day Whole Foods Challenge, congratulations! Eating whole foods is a great way to improve your health and vitality.

Planning is key. Take some time to map out your meals for the month. This will help you stay on track and avoid feeling overwhelmed. Get creative in the kitchen. There are plenty of delicious whole foods recipes out there. Experiment and find some new favorites. Don't be too hard on yourself. If you have a slip-up, don't beat yourself up. Just get back on track and keep going. Stay positive. Remember, this is a challenge to improve your health. Approach it with excitement and determination, and you'll be successful. Reach out for support. If you need some motivation or encouragement, there are plenty of people who have taken on the challenge before. One potential challenge for the 30-Day Whole Foods Challenge is giving up processed foods. Processed foods are foods that have been altered from their natural state, usually for the purpose of extending their shelf life or making them more convenient to eat. This typically means that processed foods are high in unhealthy additives like salt, sugar, and fat, and low in important nutrients like fiber and vitamins. Another potential challenge is making the switch to whole, unprocessed foods can be costly, as these foods are often more expensive than their processed counterparts. Finally, it can be difficult to find the time to cook healthy meals from scratch, especially if you are used to eating convenience foods. However, the rewards of eating a healthy, whole-food diet are well worth the effort, and with a little planning and preparation, the 30-Day Whole Foods Challenge can be a success!

## How to Follow 30-Day Whole Foods Challenges?

If you're looking to improve your diet and reset your eating habits, a 30-Day whole-foods challenge can be a great way to do it. While there are many different ways to approach a 30-Day Whole Foods challenge. When it comes to food, we all have different preferences. Some of us like our food to be cooked a certain way, while others prefer it raw. The 30-Day Whole Foods challenge is a great way to jumpstart a healthy lifestyle. By eating whole foods, you will be getting the most nutrients possible and satisfying your hunger. Some of us like to eat clean, whole foods, while others don't mind a few processed items here and there. And some of us like to challenge ourselves to eat clean for 30 days, while others find the thought of that daunting. If you're someone who likes a challenge, and you're interested in eating clean for 30 days, here are five steps to follow to make sure you're successful:

1. **Define Your Goals:** Choose a start date and commit to the challenge. Before you start your challenge, take some time to think about what you want to achieve. Are you looking to eat more nutrient-rich foods? Cut out processed foods? Reset your sugar cravings? Before you start your challenge, it's important to set a goal. Why do you want to eat clean for 30 days? What do you hope to accomplish? Having a clear goal in mind will help you stay motivated throughout the challenge. Once

you know what your goals are, you can tailor your challenge to help you reach them.

**2. Make a Plan:** Make a plan for each day, including meals and snacks. One of the keys to success with any challenge is planning. This is especially true with a 30-Day whole foods challenge, where you'll need to be extra mindful of what you're eating. Spend some time each week on meal planning and prepping so that you have healthy options on hand when you get hungry. Map out what you're going to eat each day. This doesn't have to be complicated – a simple list of meals and snacks will do. But having a plan will help you stay on track and avoid unhealthy temptations.

**3. Be Realistic:** Be realistic and Stay motivated by keeping a food journal and tracking your progress. Making the switch to a whole foods diet can be daunting, but it's important to be realistic about what you can accomplish in 30 days. Here are a few tips to help you make the transition: Start slowly and build up. If you're used to eating processed foods, your body may not be able to handle a sudden switch to a 30-Day Whole Foods diet. Start by slowly adding more whole foods to your diet and cutting back on processed foods. Don't try to do too much at once. Making big changes to your diet can be overwhelming. Take it one step at a time and focus on incorporating more whole foods into your meals and snacks. Be prepared. Have healthy snacks and meals on hand so you're not tempted to reach for unhealthy options. Planning will help you stay on track and make it more likely that you'll stick with the challenge. Be flexible. There will be days when you Slip up or don't have

**4. Shop Smart:** Fill your pantry and fridge with healthy, whole foods. This way, you won't be tempted to eat junk food. Stock your kitchen with whole foods. The 30-Day Whole Foods Challenge is a great way to save money on groceries and eat healthier. By following the challenge, you'll learn how to cook simple, healthy meals using whole foods. You'll also save money by avoiding processed foods, which are often more expensive. Plan your meals. This will help you save money by avoiding impulse purchases. Stick to a budget. Decide how much you're willing to spend on groceries each week, and then stick to it. Shop at a variety of stores. Compare prices between different stores to find the best deal.

**5. Reward Yourself:** Stay motivated by keeping a food journal and tracking your progress. Reward yourself for completing the challenge! If you've completed a 30-Day whole foods challenge, congratulations! You've committed to eating healthy and nourishing your body. Now it's time to reward yourself for all your hard work. One way to reward yourself is to treat yourself to a healthy meal or snack. You can cook yourself a nutritious meal using all the whole foods, or you can go out to eat at a restaurant that specializes in healthy fare. Another way to treat yourself is to buy yourself a new piece of workout equipment or clothing, or to sign up for a fitness class. You can also simply take some time for yourself to relax and rejuvenate. Get a massage, take a yoga class, or take a long bath. Whatever you do, make sure it's something that makes you feel good and that you enjoy. You deserve it!

## Why Are the 30-Day Whole Foods Challenges Difficult?

30-Day Whole foods challenges are difficult for a variety of reasons. For one, they require a complete overhaul of your diet, which can be tough to stick to. Additionally, they can be pricey, as buying whole, unprocessed foods can be more expensive than conventional foods. Finally, they can be time-consuming, as cooking whole foods from scratch can take longer than heating something from the freezer. However, the benefits of a 30-Day Whole Foods challenge—such as improved health, weight loss, and increased energy—are worth the effort! 30-Day Whole foods challenges can be difficult for several reasons. Here are some other reasons why a 30-Day Whole Foods challenge may be difficult for you:

- ▲ You're used to eating processed and junk food.
- ▲ You're used to eating out a lot.
- ▲ You have a busy lifestyle and don't have time to cook.
- ▲ You're not used to cooking at home.
- ▲ You don't know how to cook healthy meals.
- ▲ You're used to eating high-calorie meals.
- ▲ You're used to eating large portions.
- ▲ You're used to snacking often.
- ▲ You have a sweet tooth.
- ▲ You love salty foods.
- ▲ You're a picky eater.
- ▲ You have food allergies or intolerances.
- ▲ You have a tight budget.
- ▲ You live in a food desert.
- ▲ You don't have access to healthy food.

## Advantages of 30-Day Whole Foods

If you're considering 30-Day Whole Foods, or have already started one, you may be wondering what the benefits are. After all, it's a pretty big commitment to give up all grains, dairy, soy, legumes, alcohol, and added sugars for 30 days. So what do you get in return? If you're looking to improve your health and reset your diet, a whole-foods reset may be just what you need. Here are some advantages of resetting your diet with whole foods:

**Improved Digestion:** For many people, giving up grains, dairy, and legumes can lead to improved digestion. These food groups can be difficult to digest for some people, and eliminating them can lead to less bloating, less gas, and fewer digestive issues.

**More Energy:** When you're not constantly dealing with digestive issues, you may find that you have more energy. This is because your body can better absorb nutrients from the food you're eating.

**Clearer Skin:** For some people, eliminating dairy and sugar can lead to clearer skin.

Here are some other potential benefits of 30-Day Whole Foods

▲ You'll consume fewer toxins.
▲ You'll eat more nutrient-rich foods.
▲ You'll likely lose weight.
▲ You'll have more energy.
▲ You'll sleep better.
▲ You'll reduce inflammation.
▲ You'll detox your body.
▲ You'll improve your digestion.
▲ You'll boost your immune system.
▲ You'll lower your risk for chronic diseases.
▲ You'll feel happier and less stressed.

▲ You'll have clearer skin.
▲ You'll have stronger hair

## What Foods Are Allowed to be Eaten?

When it comes to food, there are few restrictions on what you can bring on a plane. However, the TSA does have guidelines about what types of food are allowed through security. Here are some general tips to keep in mind when packing food for your next flight:

▲ All liquids, gels, and aerosols must be in containers that are 3.4 ounces (100 milliliters) or less and placed in a single, clear, quart-sized bag.

▲ Solid food items are generally allowed through security.

▲ If you are bringing a baby or toddler with you on your flight, you are allowed to bring baby food and formula through security.

▲ If you are traveling with special dietary needs, you are allowed to bring food items that are necessary for your health and well-being.

So, what types of food are allowed on a plane? Anything that is not a liquid or gel is allowed. There are a variety of food items that are allowed to be

eaten. However, not all foods are allowed to be eaten in every country. For example, in some countries, pork is not allowed to be eaten. In others, beef is not allowed. It is important to check with the local authorities to find out what specific food items are allowed to be eaten in the country that you are visiting.

## What Foods Are Not Allowed to be Eaten?

There are a few different types of food that are not allowed to be eaten. The first type is poisonous food. This includes things like poisonous mushrooms, fish that have been poisonous, and so on. The second type is food that is contaminated. This includes food that has been tainted with bacteria or other contaminants. The third type is food that is unhealthy. This includes food that is high in saturated fat, sugar, or salt.

**Poisonous:** There are many reasons why poisonous food is not allowed to be eaten. For one, they can be incredibly dangerous to our health. Poisonous food can contain harmful toxins that can cause serious illness or even death. Additionally, poisonous food can be difficult to digest and can cause digestive problems. Finally, poisonous food can also be environmentally harmful, as it can contaminate water supplies and soil.

**Contaminated:** There are many reasons why contaminated food is not allowed to be eaten. The main reason is that it can make you sick. Contaminated food can contain bacteria, viruses, or toxins that can cause food poisoning, diarrhea, or other serious illnesses. Another reason why contaminated food is not allowed to be eaten is that it can spread diseases. If you eat contaminated food, you can spread the bacteria or viruses to other

people. This can cause a foodborne illness outbreak. Contaminated food can also contain harmful chemicals. These chemicals can be toxic and can cause serious health problems. So, it is important to avoid eating contaminated food. If you think you have eaten contaminated food, you should see a doctor right away.

**Unhealthy:** Unhealthy food is not allowed to be eaten because it can lead to several health problems. These include obesity, heart disease, high blood pressure, and type 2 diabetes. Unhealthy food is also high in calories and low in nutrients, which can contribute to weight gain and other health problems. If you are taking Coumadin (warfarin), it is important to be aware of foods that can interact with the medication and affect its effectiveness. Here are some foods that you should avoid while taking Coumadin:

**Green leafy vegetables:** These vegetables contain high levels of vitamin K, which can interact with Coumadin and reduce its effectiveness. Examples of green leafy vegetables to avoid include spinach, kale, and collard greens.

**Cauliflower:** Like green leafy vegetables, cauliflower also contains high levels of vitamin K.

**Soybean products:** Soybeans and soybean products (tofu, soy milk, etc.) contain a substance known as genistein, which can interact with Coumadin and reduce its effectiveness.

**Alcohol:** Alcohol can interact with Coumadin and increase the risk of bleeding.

**Grapefruit:** Grapefruit contains a substance that can interact with Coumadin. So, it is good for health to avoid grapefruit while taking Coumadin.

## Suggestions and Cautions

If you're considering doing a 30-Day Whole Foods challenge, congratulations! This is a great way to reset your body and give your digestive system a break. Here are a few suggestions to help you make the most of your challenge:

**Plan ahead:** This challenge is not something you want to try to wing. Decide which 30 days you're going to do the challenge and make a grocery list accordingly. The 30-Day Whole Foods Challenge is a great way to jumpstart your healthy eating habits. By planning and being prepared, you can make the most of the challenge and see amazing results. Meal planning is key to success on any diet, but especially on a 30-Day Whole Foods Challenge. Stock your pantry and fridge with healthy, whole foods ingredients so you always have something to eat. Here are a few tips to help you plan and make the most of the challenge:

▲ Decide what your goals are. What do you hope to accomplish by taking on the challenge? Whether it's weight loss, more energy, or simply eating healthier, having a clear goal in mind will help you stay on track.

▲ Make a list of all the foods you'll need. This includes everything from staples like fruits, vegetables, and whole grains to more specific items like almond milk and quinoa.

▲ Stock your pantry and fridge. Before the challenge begins, make sure you have all the foods you need on hand. This will make it easier to stick to the challenge and avoid any temptation to cheat.

**Stick to whole, unprocessed foods.** This means no pre-packaged meals or snacks, no processed meats or cheeses, and no artificial sweeteners. If you're like me, you love a good challenge. That's why I've decided to do the 30-Day Whole Foods Challenge. For 30 days, I'm going to eat nothing but whole foods. That means no processed foods, no artificial ingredients, and no added sugar. I know this is going to be a challenge, but I'm up for it. I want to see how my body feels when I'm eating nothing but whole foods. I'm also curious to see if I have more energy and feel better overall.

**Cook at home as much as possible.** Eating out can be tricky on 30-Day Whole Foods, so it's best to cook at home as much as you can. One of the best things about cooking at home is that you know exactly what's going into your food. No more wondering about hidden ingredients or added sugars - when you cook at home, you have complete control over your ingredients. Another great thing about cooking at home is that it can save you money. Eating out all the time can get expensive, but cooking at home is a great way to save some cash.

**Get creative with your meals.** Just because you're avoiding processed foods doesn't mean you have to eat boring meals. Get creative with your recipes and experiment with new ingredients. This can be a great way to jumpstart your healthy eating habits and see some real results. To get started, simply commit to eating only whole foods for 30 days. This means no processed or refined foods, no fast food, and no sugary drinks. Fill your diet with fresh fruits and vegetables, whole grains, lean proteins, and healthy fats. To make sure you stick to your goals, plan your meals and stock your kitchen with healthy ingredients. Meal prep can help you stay on track, and it's also a great way to save time and money. Throughout the challenge, pay attention to how you're feeling. Do you have more energy? Are you sleeping better? Are your skin and hair looking healthier? Be sure to celebrate your successes, no matter how big or small.

Here are a few things to keep in mind as you embark on this challenge:

▲ Don't be too hard on yourself. This challenge is about making small, sustainable changes. If you slip up, don't beat yourself up. Just get back on track and keep going.

▲ Be prepared for cravings. When you first cut out processed foods, you may find yourself craving them more than usual. This is normal! Stick to your plan and the cravings will eventually subside.

▲ Drink plenty of water. Water is essential for good health.

▲ Don't go into this challenge expecting to lose a ton of weight. While you may lose some weight, the goal of this challenge is to eat healthier, not necessarily to lose weight.

▲ You may be surprised at how difficult it is to give up some of your favorite unhealthy foods. Be prepared for some temptations and cravings.

▲ Eating out can be tricky on this challenge. It's best to cook at home as much as possible.

▲ You may need to get creative with your meals. Eating the same thing every day can get boring.

▲ You may not have as much energy at first.

# 4-Week Meal Plan

## Week 1

**Day 1:**
Breakfast: Onion and Tomato Frittata
Lunch: Cheesy Zucchini
Snack: Garlicky Chicken Skewers
Dinner: Chicken and Cucumber Salad
Dessert: Special Vanilla Apple Cake

**Day 2:**
Breakfast: Turmeric Bell Pepper & Onion Frittata
Lunch: Kohlrabi with Creamy Mushroom
Snack: Crispy Kale Chips
Dinner: Pork and Veggie Stew
Dessert: Vanilla Hemp Hearts

**Day 3:**
Breakfast: Egg and Beef Casserole with Kale & Sweet Potato
Lunch: Spinach and Strawberry Salad with Cheese
Snack: Rosemary Crackers
Dinner: Creamy Tilapia
Dessert: Rhubarb Strawberry Mousse

**Day 4:**
Breakfast: Hard-Boiled Eggs
Lunch: Spicy Cabbage and Squash Kimchi
Snack: Coconut Sesame Seed Crackers
Dinner: Chicken and Veggie Stew
Dessert: Pecans Squash Pudding

**Day 5:**
Breakfast: Nutty Coconut Pear Porridge
Lunch: Cheese-Crusted Green Beans
Snack: Chocolate Coconut Bars
Dinner: Beef and Plantains Stew
Dessert: Delicious Chestnut Cream

**Day 6:**
Breakfast: Raspberries Rhubarb Pearls Porridge
Lunch: Creamy Cauliflower Mash
Snack: Roasted Almonds with Herbs
Dinner: Lemony Coconut Cod Curry
Dessert: Mixed Fruit Bowls

**Day 7:**
Breakfast: Coconut Pumpkin Muffins
Lunch: Herbed Portobello Mushrooms
Snack: Grilled Mushrooms Stuffed with Onion Dip
Dinner: Chicken and Rutabaga Soup
Dessert: Easy Chocolate Parfait

## Week 2

**Day 1:**
Breakfast: Keto Green Smoothie with Chia Seeds
Lunch: Minty Snap Peas
Snack: Chestnuts Apricot Bites
Dinner: Apple & Cranberry Stuffed Pork Chops
Dessert: Mulberry and Dates Cupcakes

**Day 2:**
Breakfast: Eggs Benedict with Bacon
Lunch: Easy Okra and Tomatoes with Crispy Bacon
Snack: Turkey Stuffed Mushroom
Dinner: Tangy Minute Steaks
Dessert: Tropical Fruit with Coconut Cream

**Day 3:**
Breakfast: Cheese Yogurt Soufflé
Lunch: Chard and Cashews Side Dish
Snack: Spicy Mushroom and Broccoli Skewers
Dinner: Grilled Lime Chicken Wings
Dessert: Tasty Banana Pancakes

**Day 4:**
Breakfast: Chocolate and Chia Seeds Pudding
Lunch: Grilled Cajun Veggies
Snack: Turkey & Tomato Stuffed Zucchini Rolls
Dinner: Cajun Garlicky Pulled Pork
Dessert: Cherry, Chocolate and Coconut Bark

**Day 5:**
Breakfast: Chicken and Zucchini Frittata
Lunch: Avocado Green Beans Salad
Snack: Cauliflower and Turkey Bites
Dinner: Tropical Shrimp Stew
Dessert: Mango and Passion Fruit Sorbet

**Day 6:**
Breakfast: Chicken-Tomato Omelet
Lunch: Delicious Asparagus Mash
Snack: Avocado& Cucumber on Watermelon Circles
Dinner: Cilantro Chicken with Mayo-Avocado Sauce
Dessert: Green Apple and Spinach Smoothie

**Day 7:**
Breakfast: Cheese Tomato Bowls with Spinach
Lunch: Roasted Spiced Summer Squash
Snack: Bacon-Cucumber Rolls
Dinner: Turkey Patties with Cucumber Salsa
Dessert: Special Vanilla Apple Cake

## Week 3

**Day 1:**
Breakfast: Pear Breakfast Bowls with Walnuts
Lunch: Easy Spinach Omelet
Snack: Simple Cabbage Chips
Dinner: Herbed Pork Loin Roast with Bacon
Dessert: Rhubarb Strawberry Mousse

**Day 2:**
Breakfast: Beef and Sausage Burgers
Lunch: Zucchini and Parsley Mash
Snack: Bacon-Wrapped Enoki Mushrooms
Dinner: Cod in Ginger Tamarind Sauce
Dessert: Vanilla Hemp Hearts

**Day 3:**
Breakfast: Ham, Mushroom and Egg Scramble
Lunch: Carrot Mash
Snack: Spicy Sweet Potatoes Chips
Dinner: Lemon-Garlic Chicken with Potatoes
Dessert: Delicious Chestnut Cream

**Day 4:**
Breakfast: Coconut Porridge
Lunch: Easy Steamed Potatoes
Snack: Homemade Mexican Mole
Dinner: Herbed Beef Roast
Dessert: Pecans Squash Pudding

**Day 5:**
Breakfast: Chorizo and Mushroom Breakfast with Egg
Lunch: Potato and Carrot Salad
Snack: Foil Wrapped Potatoes and Green Beans
Dinner: Coconut Prawns and Okra
Dessert: Mixed Fruit Bowls

**Day 6:**
Breakfast: Spicy Chicken Waffles
Lunch: Sautéed Cabbage, Pear, and Onion
Snack: Grilled Garlicky Yellow Squash
Dinner: Lemon Baked Whole Chicken
Dessert: Mulberry and Dates Cupcakes

**Day 7:**
Breakfast: Beef and Squash Skillet with Eggs
Lunch: Cauliflower, Sweet Potato and Peas Bowl
Snack: Stir-Fry Eggplant
Dinner: Beef Pot Roast and Potato Stew
Dessert: Easy Chocolate Parfait

## Week 4

**Day 1:**
Breakfast: Onion and Tomato Frittata
Lunch: Chinese-Style Green Bean Stir Fry
Snack: Grilled Lemony Romaine Lettuce
Dinner: Tasty Baked Tilapia
Dessert: Tropical Fruit with Coconut Cream

**Day 2:**
Breakfast: Nutty Coconut Pear Porridge
Lunch: Cheesy Zucchini
Snack: Garlicky Chicken Skewers
Dinner: Tasty Turkey Legs
Dessert: Tasty Banana Pancakes

**Day 3:**
Breakfast: Egg and Beef Casserole with Kale & Sweet Potato
Lunch: Spicy Cabbage and Squash Kimchi
Snack: Chocolate Coconut Bars
Dinner: Beef and Potato Hash
Dessert: Cherry, Chocolate and Coconut Bark

**Day 4:**
Breakfast: Turmeric Bell Pepper & Onion Frittata
Lunch: Spinach and Strawberry Salad with Cheese
Snack: Crispy Kale Chips
Dinner: Salmon with Potatoes & Broccoli
Dessert: Mango and Passion Fruit Sorbet

**Day 5:**
Breakfast: Raspberries Rhubarb Pearls Porridge
Lunch: Kohlrabi with Creamy Mushroom
Snack: Rosemary Crackers
Dinner: Grilled Juicy Chicken
Dessert: Green Apple and Spinach Smoothie

**Day 6:**
Breakfast: Coconut Pumpkin Muffins
Lunch: Creamy Cauliflower Mash
Snack: Roasted Almonds with Herbs
Dinner: Spicy Barbequed Steak
Dessert: Vanilla Hemp Hearts

**Day 7:**
Breakfast: Eggs Benedict with Bacon
Lunch: Cheese-Crusted Green Beans
Snack: Chestnuts Apricot Bites
Dinner: BBQ Rack Ribs On the Grill
Dessert: Pecans Squash Pudding

# Chapter 1 Breakfast Recipes

# Onion and Tomato Frittata

**Prep Time: 10 minutes | Cook Time: 8 minutes | Servings: 2**

**Ingredients:**

4 eggs

1 tomato, chopped

1 red onion, diced

¼ tsp garlic powder

Pinch of cayenne pepper

Pinch of black pepper

1½ cups water

**Instructions:**

1. Add water to the Instant Pot and lower the trivet. 2. Grease a baking dish with some cooking spray. 3. Beat the eggs along with the garlic powder, cayenne, and black pepper. 4. Add tomatoes and onions and stir to combine well. 5. Transfer the mixture to the greased baking dish. 6. Place the baking dish on top of the trivet and close the lid. 7. Turn clockwise to seal and press "MANUAL". Cook on HIGH for 8 minutes. 8. After the beep, press "KEEP WARM/CANCEL". 9. When the Instant Pot is off, move the pressure release handle from "Sealing" to "Venting" to do a quick pressure release. 10. Open the lid carefully and remove the baking dish from the pot. 11. Serve and enjoy!

**Per Serving:** Calories 293; Fat 19.46g; Sodium 213mg; Carbs 9.85g; Fiber 1.7g; Sugar 5.26g; Protein 19g

# Hard-Boiled Eggs

**Prep Time: 3 minutes | Cook Time: 7 minutes | Servings: 4**

**Ingredients:**

8 Eggs

1 cup of Water

**Instructions:**

1. Pour the water into the Instant Pot and place the eggs inside. Put the lid on and turn it clockwise to seal. After you hear the chime, press the "MANUAL" button. Cook on HIGH pressure for 3 minutes. 2. After you hear the beeping sound, press "KEEP WARM/CANCEL" and turn the Instant Pot off. Do a quick pressure release by moving the handle from "Sealing" to "Venting". Open the lid and be careful not to put your hands near the steam. 3. Prepare an ice bath and drop the hardboiled eggs into it to speed up the process of cooling. 4. Serve and enjoy!

**Per Serving:** Calories 259; Fat 19.28g; Sodium 206mg; Carbs 2.03g; Fiber 0g; Sugar 1.3g; Protein 17.93g

# Turmeric Bell Pepper & Onion Frittata

**Prep Time: 7 minutes | Cook Time: 8 minutes | Servings: 2**

**Ingredients:**

3 eggs

¼ cup diced bell pepper

¼ cup diced onion

2 tbsps almond milk

¼ tsp garlic powder

Pinch of turmeric powder

1½ cups water

**Instructions:**

1. Pour the water into the Instant Pot and lower the trivet. Grease a small baking dish with some cooking spray. 2. In a bowl, beat the eggs along with the almond milk, turmeric, and garlic powder. 3. Add onions and bell peppers and stir well to combine. 4. Pour the mixture into the greased baking dish and place it on top of the trivet. 5. Close the lid of the Instant Pot and turn it clockwise. The chiming sound means it is sealed properly. 6. Select "MANUAL" and set the cooking time to 8 minutes. Cook on HIGH. 7. After the timer goes off, press "KEEP WARM/CANCEL" to turn the Instant Pot off. 8. Release the pressure quickly by moving the pressure release handle from "Sealing" to "Venting". 9. Keep your hands away from the steam to avoid burning yourself. 10. Open the lid Carefully and remove the dish from the pot. 11. Serve and enjoy!

**Per Serving:** Calories 204; Fat 14.49g; Sodium 158mg; Carbs 3.69g; Fiber 0.4g; Sugar 1.88g; Protein 13.79g

# Chicken-Tomato Omelet

**Prep Time: 10 minutes | Cook time: 3 hours Servings: 2**

**Ingredients:**

1 ounce rotisserie chicken, shredded

1 teaspoon mustard

1 tablespoon homemade mayonnaise

1 tomato, chopped

2 bacon slices, cooked and crumbled

4 eggs

1 small avocado, pitted, peeled and chopped

Salt and black pepper to the taste

**Instructions:**

1. In a bowl, mix the eggs with salt and pepper and whisk. 2. Add chicken, avocado, tomato, bacon, mayo and mustard, toss, transfer to your Crockpot, cover and cook on Low for 3 hours. 3. Divide between plates and serve. 4. Enjoy!

**Per Serving:** Calories 592; Fat 48.01g; Sodium 432mg; Carbs 15.72g; Fiber 8g; Sugar 5.03g; Protein 27.21g

# Egg and Beef Casserole with Kale & Sweet Potato

**Prep Time: 10 minutes | Cook Time: 30 minutes | Servings: 4**

**Ingredients:**

8 ounces ground beef

6 eggs, beaten

¾ cup sliced leeks

¾ cup chopped kale

1 sweet potato, peeled and shredded

1 garlic clove, minced

1 tbsp coconut oil

Pinch of pepper

1½ cups water

**Instructions:**

1. Grease a baking dish with some cooking spray and set aside. 2. Add coconut oil to the Instant Pot and set it to "SAUTE". When melted, add the leeks and cook for about 2 minutes. 3. Add the garlic and cook for 30 seconds or so. Add the beef and cook for a few more minutes, until browned. 4. Transfer to a bowl. Add the remaining ingredients and stir well to combine. 5. Pour the water into the Instant Pot and lower the trivet. Pour the egg and beef mixture into the greased baking dish and place on top of the trivet. 6. Close the lid and turn clockwise to seal. Select "MANUAL" and set the cooking time to 25 minutes. Cook on HIGH. 7. After the beep, press "KEEP WARM/CANCEL" to turn the Instant Pot off. 8. Release the pressure quickly by moving the handle to "Venting". Be careful not to burn yourself and open the lid. 9. Remove the baking dish from the pot carefully. 10. Serve and enjoy!

**Per Serving:** Calories 362; Fat 24.26g; Sodium 195mg; Carbs 5.46g; Fiber 0.6g; Sugar 2.28g; Protein 29.2g

# Keto Green Smoothie with Chia Seeds

**Prep Time: 10 minutes | Cook Time: 0 minutes | Servings: 1**

**Ingredients:**

1 oz. spinach

1½ cups almond milk

1.6 oz. celery

1.6 oz. cucumber

⅐ oz. avocado

10 drops liquid stevia

1 tablespoon coconut oil

½ teaspoon chia seeds, for garnishing

**Instructions:**

1. Add the spinach and milk to your blender and blend until smooth. 2. Add the remaining ingredients to the blender and blend again until smooth and creamy. 3. Pour into a glass, sprinkle with the chia seeds and serve.

**Per Serving:** Calories 366; Fat 26.42g; Sodium 217mg; Carbs 21.2g; Fiber 1.9g; Sugar 19.86g; Protein 13g

# Chocolate and Chia Seeds Pudding

## Prep Time: 10 minutes | Cook time: 3 hours and 15 minutes | Servings: 2

**Ingredients:**

2 tablespoons coffee

2 cups water

⅓ cup chia seeds

1 tablespoon stevia

1 tablespoon vanilla extract

2 tablespoons unsweetened chocolate chips

¼ cup coconut cream

**Instructions:**

1. Heat up a small pot with the water over medium heat, bring to a boil, add coffee, simmer for 15 minutes, take off heat and strain into your Crockpot. 2. Add vanilla extract, coconut cream, stevia, chocolate chips and chia seeds, stir well, cover and cook on Low for 3 hours. 3. Divide between bowls and serve cold for breakfast. Enjoy!

**Per Serving:** Calories 227; Fat 10.85g; Sodium 35mg; Carbs 28.21g; Fiber 1.7g; Sugar 20.19g; Protein 1.93g

# Coconut Pumpkin Muffins

## Prep Time: 15 minutes | Cook Time: 30 minutes | Servings: 5

1-cup coconut flour

½ cup pumpkin puree

2 pastured eggs

½ tsp cinnamon

½ tsp coconut oil

½ tsp vanilla extract

½ tsp baking powder

½ tsp baking soda

½ tbsp almond butter

¾ tsp pumpkin spice

**Instructions:**

1. Preheat an oven and prepare muffin paper cups. 2. Melt almond butter over low heat, and then set aside. 3. Combine coconut flour, cinnamon, baking powder, baking soda, and pumpkin spice in a bowl. Mix well. 4. Crack the eggs in a bowl then add coconut oil, vanilla extract, and pumpkin spice. Using a hand mixer, blend the ingredients until smooth and creamy. 5. Add the dry mixture into the liquid one, then continue to whisk. 6. Finally, add pumpkin puree and blend using a hand mixer. 7. Pour the batter into each muffin paper cups then bake for approximately 30 minutes. 8. Once the muffins are cooked, remove from the oven and arrange on a serving dish. 9. Serve warm.

**Per Serving:** Calories 146; Fat 11.13g; Sodium 252mg; Carbs 4.9g; Fiber 1.6g; Sugar 1.84g; Protein 7.81g

# Chicken and Zucchini Frittata

**Prep Time: 10 minutes | Cook time: 5 hours | Servings: 5**

**Ingredients:**

7 eggs

3 tablespoons almond flour

1 tablespoon olive oil

A pinch of salt and black pepper

2 zucchinis, grated

½ cup coconut cream

1 teaspoon fennel seeds

1 teaspoon oregano, dried

1 pound chicken meat, ground

**Instructions:**

1. In a bowl, mix the eggs with flour, salt, pepper, cream, zucchini, fennel, oregano and meat, whisk well, pour into your Crockpot after you've greased it with the oil, cover and cook on Low for 5 hours. 2. Slice frittata, divide between plates and serve for breakfast. 3. Enjoy!

**Per Serving:** Calories 437; Fat 32.35g; Sodium 237mg; Carbs 4.51g; Fiber 1g; Sugar 1.41g; Protein 31.83g

# Cheese Yogurt Soufflé

**Prep Time: 10 minutes | Cook Time: 25 minutes | Servings: 2**

**Ingredients:**

4 tbsps almond flour

½ tsp mustard

¼ tsp black pepper

½ cup yogurt

1 cup shredded cheese

3 pastured eggs

**Instructions:**

1. Preheat an oven to 350°F then prepares 4 soufflé cups. 2. Crack the eggs and place the yolks and the egg whites in the separate bowl. 3. Place the almond flour; mustard, cheese, and black pepper in a bowl then stir until well mixed. 4. Pour yogurt and egg yolks over the almond flour mixture then mix until incorporated. 5. Using an electric mixer to whisk the egg whites until fluffy and reach the soft peak. 6. Slowly fold the egg whites into the almond mixture then stir until completely incorporated. 7. Divide the batter into 4 and pour into the prepared soufflé cups. 8. Bake for about 25 mins until well cooked and lightly brown. 9. Remove the soufflé from the oven and serve right away.

**Per Serving:** Calories 493; Fat 37.69g; Sodium 591mg; Carbs 5.64g; Fiber 0.4g; Sugar 4.28g; Protein 32.32g

# Nutty Coconut Pear Porridge

## Prep Time: 3 minutes | Cook Time: 3 minutes | Servings: 1

**Ingredients:**

½ cup ground walnuts

1 ounces coconut flakes

1 pear, diced

½ cup coconut milk

**Instructions:**

1. Place all of the ingredients in your Instant Pot and stir well to combine. Put the lid on. 2. Turn clockwise to seal, and after you hear the chime hit "MANUAL". Use the "+" and "-" buttons and set the cooking time to 3 minutes. Make sure to cook on HIGH pressure. 3. When the timer goes off, press "KEEP WARM/CANCEL" and move the handle to "Venting" for a quick pressure release. Open the lid but keep your hands away from the steam to avoid burning. 4. Then transfer the mixture to a serving bowl and stir once again to combine. Enjoy!

**Per Serving:** Calories 543; Fat 54.75g; Sodium 49mg; Carbs 13.19g; Fiber 5.6g; Sugar 5.79g; Protein 9.04g

# Beef and Sausage Burgers

## Prep Time: 30 minutes | Cook Time:20 minutes | Servings: 4

**Ingredients:**

8 bacon slices; chopped and cooked

5 eggs

1 lb. beef; ground

½ cup sausage; ground

3 sun-dried tomatoes; chopped

2 tbsp. almond meal

2 tsp. basil

2 tbsp. coconut oil

1 tsp. garlic; minced

**Instructions:**

1. In a bowl; mix beef with garlic, basil, tomatoes, almond meal and 1 egg, stir well and shape 4 burgers. 2. Heat up a grill over medium high heat, add burgers, cook them for 5 minutes on each side, transfer to plates and leave them aside. 3. Heat up a pan over medium high heat, add sausage, cook until it's done and divide into burgers. Add cooked bacon on top of sausages and leave aside for now. 4. Heat up a pan with the coconut oil over medium high heat, crack one egg at a time, fry them well and divide them on burgers.

**Per Serving:** Calories 724; Fat 54.09g; Sodium 506mg; Carbs 6.8g; Fiber 1.2g; Sugar 1.28g; Protein 51.24g

# Cheese Tomato Bowls with Spinach

**Prep Time: 10 minutes | Cook time: 6 hours | Servings: 6**

**Ingredients:**

10 ounces feta cheese, crumbled
1 green bell pepper, chopped
¼ cup scallions, chopped
15 ounces canned tomatoes, chopped
1 cup fresh tomato puree
½ cup water

¼ teaspoon cumin powder
½ teaspoon turmeric powder
½ teaspoon smoked paprika
A pinch of salt and black pepper
¼ teaspoon chili powder
3 cups spinach leaves, torn

**Instructions:**

1. In your Crockpot, mix cheese with bell pepper, scallions, tomatoes, tomato puree, water, cumin, turmeric, paprika, salt, pepper and chili powder, stir, cover and cook on Low for 6 hours. 2. Add spinach, toss well, divide this into bowls and serve for breakfast. 3. Enjoy!
**Per Serving:** Calories 165; Fat 10.49g; Sodium 544mg; Carbs 10.77g; Fiber 3g; Sugar 6.72g; Protein 8.85g

# Chorizo and Mushroom Breakfast with Egg

**Prep Time: 20 minutes | Cook Time: 26 minutes | Servings: 2**

**Ingredients:**

1 small avocado; peeled, pitted and chopped
½ cup beef stock
1 lb. chorizo; chopped
2 poblano peppers; chopped
1 cup kale; chopped
8 mushrooms; chopped

½ yellow onion; chopped
3 garlic cloves; minced
½ cup cilantro; chopped
4 bacon slices; chopped
4 eggs

**Instructions:**

1. Heat up a pan over medium heat, add chorizo and bacon, stir and cook until they are browned. 2. Add garlic, peppers and onions, stir and cook for 6 minutes more. 3. Add stock, mushrooms and kale, stir and cook for 4 minutes more. 4. Make holes in this mix, crack an egg in each, place in the oven at 350°F and bake for 12 minutes. 5. Divide this mix on plates, sprinkle cilantro and avocado on top and serve.
**Per Serving:** Calories 1735; Fat 141.75g; Sodium 3276mg; Carbs 30.44g; Fiber 9.4g; Sugar 10.53g; Protein 85.62g

# Pear Breakfast Bowls with Walnuts

## Prep Time: 10 minutes | Cook time: 9 hours | Servings: 2

**Ingredients:**

1 pear, cored and chopped

½ teaspoon maple extract

2 cups coconut milk

½ cup flax meal

½ teaspoon vanilla extract

1 tablespoon stevia

¼ cup walnuts, chopped

Cooking spray

**Instructions:**

1. Spray your Crockpot with some cooking spray, add coconut milk, maple extract, flax meal, pear, stevia and vanilla extract, stir, cover and cook on Low for 9 hours. 2. Divide it into breakfast bowls and serve with chopped walnuts on top. 3. Enjoy!

**Per Serving:** Calories 261; Fat 15.71g; Sodium 127mg; Carbs 20.1g; Fiber 0.7g; Sugar 13.71g; Protein 10.59g

# Beef and Squash Skillet with Eggs

## Prep Time: 10 minutes | Cook Time: 25 minutes | Servings: 3

**Ingredients:**

15 oz. beef; ground

2 tbsp. ghee

3 garlic cloves; minced

2 celery stalks; chopped

1 yellow onion; chopped

A pinch of sea salt

White pepper to the taste

½ tsp. coriander; ground

1 tsp. cumin; ground

1 tsp. garam masala

½ butternut squash; chopped and already cooked

3 eggs

1 small avocado; peeled, pitted and chopped

15 oz. spinach

**Instructions:**

1. Put spinach in a heatproof bowl; place in your microwave and cook for 1 minute. 2. Squeeze spinach and leave it aside. 3. Heat up a pan with the ghee over medium heat, add onion, garlic, celery, a pinch of salt and white pepper, stir and cook for 3 minutes. 4. Add beef, cumin, garam masala and coriander, stir and cook for a few minutes more. 5. Add squash flesh and spinach, stir and make 3 holes in this mix. 6. Crack an egg into each, cover pan, place in the oven at 375°F and bake for 15 minutes. 7. Divide this mix on plates and serve with avocado on top.

**Per Serving:** Calories 790; Fat 62.85g; Sodium 333mg; Carbs 23.27g; Fiber 9.1g; Sugar 8.19g; Protein 36.28g

# Spicy Chicken Waffles

**Ingredients:**

1½ cups chicken; cooked and shredded

½ cup hot sauce

1 cup almond flour

2 green onions; chopped

½ cup tapioca flour

2 eggs

6 tbsp. coconut flour

A pinch of cayenne pepper

¾ tsp. baking soda

1 tsp. garlic powder

1 cup coconut milk

¼ cup ghee+ some more for the waffle iron

A pinch of sea salt

**Instructions:**

1. In a bowl, mix almond flour with tapioca flour, coconut one, baking soda, garlic powder and a pinch of salt and stir well. 2. Add chicken, hot sauce, green onions, eggs, milk and ¼ cup ghee and blend using your mixer. 3. Pour some of the batter into your greased waffle iron, close the lid and make your waffle. 4. Repeat with the rest of the batter, divide waffles between plates and serve them in the morning.

**Per Serving:** Calories 450; Fat 24.98g; Sodium 396mg; Carbs 39.03g; Fiber 2.8g; Sugar 14.82g; Protein 17.77g

# Ham, Mushroom and Egg Scramble

**Ingredients:**

2 tbsp. ghee

¼ cup coconut milk

3 eggs

2 oz. smoked ham; chopped

3 oz. mushrooms; sliced

1 cup arugula; torn

A pinch of black pepper

**Instructions:**

1. Heat up a pan with half of the ghee over medium heat, add mushrooms, stir and cook for 3 minutes. 2. Add ham, stir; cook for 2-3 minutes more and transfer everything to a plate. 3. In a bowl; mix eggs with coconut milk and black pepper and whisk well. 4. Heat up the pan with the rest of the ghee over medium heat, add eggs, spread into the pan, cook for a couple of minutes, start stirring and cook until eggs are completely done. 5. Transfer this to a serving bowl; add mushrooms mix on top and arugula. Toss everything to coat well and serve right away.

**Per Serving:** Calories 502; Fat 32.1g; Sodium 601mg; Carbs 15.79g; Fiber 1.8g; Sugar 9.42g; Protein 37.96g

# Raspberries Rhubarb Pearls Porridge

Prep Time: 10minutes | Cook Time: 31minutes | Servings: 3

## Ingredients

**Raspberry-Rhubarb Sauce:**

1 teaspoon coconut oil

2 cups frozen chopped rhubarb

1 tablespoon water, or as needed (optional)

1 cup raspberries

1 packet stevia powder, or to taste

**Porridge:**

2 dates, pitted and chopped

2 cups water, or as needed

¾ cup small tapioca pearls

⅔ cup coconut milk

1 tablespoon maca powder

1 tablespoon vanilla extract

1 packet stevia powder, or to taste (optional)

## Instructions:

1. Use coconut oil to coat a saucepan; put on moderate heat. Put in rhubarb and cook for 10 minutes until it begins to soften, putting in more water if necessary. Stir into rhubarb with 1 packet stevia powder and raspberries. Cook for 5-10 minutes until the sauce is smooth. 2. In a pot, add water until halfway full, then bring to a boil. Put in tapioca and simmer on moderate heat about one minute while stirring frequently. Turn heat to low and keep simmering for 5-8 minutes, until tapioca is totally translucent. 3. In a blender, process vanilla extract, maca powder, dates and coconut milk until smooth. 4. Use a fine-mesh strainer to strain tapioca porridges and put back to the pot on low heat. Stir in 1 packet of stevia powder and coconut mixture. Simmer for 5 minutes longer, until liquid is absorbed. 5. Put porridge to 3 wine glasses and pour raspberry-rhubarb sauce on top.

Per Serving: Calories 490; Fat 4.23g; Sodium 36mg; Carbs 113.18g; Fiber 7.1g; Sugar 71.86g; Protein 3.58g

# Coconut Porridge

Prep Time: 16 minutes | Cook Time: 6 minutes | Servings: 3

## Ingredients:

1 big plantain; peeled and mashed

¼ cup flax meal

2 cups coconut milk

¾ cup almond meal

1 tsp. cinnamon; powder

A pinch of cloves; ground

½ tsp. ginger powder

A pinch of nutmeg; ground

Maple syrup for serving

Some unsweetened coconut flakes for serving

## Instructions:

1. In a small pan, mix plantain with flax meal, almond meal, coconut milk, cinnamon, cloves, ginger and nutmeg, stir well, bring to a simmer over medium heat and cook for about 6 minutes. 2. Divide your porridge into bowls, top with coconut flakes and maple syrup and serve.

Per Serving: Calories 384; Fat 10.86g; Sodium 419mg; Carbs 62.39g; Fiber 3.4g; Sugar 38.55g; Protein 12.03g

# Eggs Benedict with Bacon

## Prep Time: 10 minutes | Cook Time: 20 minutes | Servings: 2

**Ingredients:**

For the Sauce:

2 egg yolks

1 teaspoon lemon juice

2 tablespoon butter, melted

For the Eggs:

1 tablespoon white vinegar

Salt, to taste

4 eggs

1 pinch paprika

1 pitch salt

4 rolls

4 slices Canadian bacon, fried

1 teaspoon chives

**Instructions:**

To prepare the sauce: 1. Whisk the egg yolks in a saucepan and mix in the lemon juice. Heat on very low heat and whisk continuously until the eggs has thickened. 2. Mix in the melted butter keeping the heat on low. If the heat is not extremely low, the eggs will cook and become scrambled. Alternatively, you can use a double broiler to prepare the sauce. 3. When done, remove from the heat, sprinkle with the paprika and salt and set aside. If the sauce becomes too thick, mix in a tbsp of water.

To prepare the eggs: 1. Fill a pot with water up to 3 inches and bring to the boil. Reduce the heat to a simmer and add the vinegar and salt. 2. Using a wooden spoon, stir in one direction a few times to create a whirlpool. Gently lower a cracked egg into the whirlpool and leave it to cook for about 5 minutes. Gently take out the egg and place it on a plate lined with a paper towel. Repeat the same with the remaining eggs. 3. To serve, place an egg on each of the rolls, drizzle with the sauce and sprinkle with the chives, salt, and pepper.

Per Serving: Calories 715; Fat 40.05g; Sodium 1148mg; Carbs 45.78g; Fiber 1.8g; Sugar 7.37g; Protein 40.6g

# Chapter 2 Vegetable and Sides Recipes

# Cheesy Zucchini

<u>Prep Time: 15 minutes | Cook Time: 5 minutes | Servings: 1</u>

**Ingredients:**

1 tablespoon olive oil

1 tablespoon basil; chopped.

¼ cup asiago cheese; shaved

1 teaspoon red pepper flakes

1 tablespoon garlic; minced

1 tablespoon red bell pepper; chopped.

¼ cup parmesan; grated

3 tablespoons ghee

2 cups zucchini; cut with a spiralizer

Salt and black pepper to the taste.

**Instructions:**

1. Heat up a pan with the oil and ghee over medium heat; add garlic, bell pepper and pepper flakes; stir and cook them for 1 minute. 2. Add zucchini noodles; stir and cook for 2 minutes more. 3. Add basil, parmesan, salt and pepper; stir and cook for a few seconds more. 4. Take off heat; transfer to a bowl and serve for lunch with asiago cheese on top.

**Per Serving:** Calories 390; Fat 25.4g; Sodium 452mg; Carbs 23.14g; Fiber 3.4g; Sugar 9.02g; Protein 20.46g

# Carrot Mash

<u>Prep Time: 10 minutes | Cook Time: 4 minutes | Servings: 4</u>

**Ingredients:**

1 tsp Turmeric Powder

¼ tsp Black Pepper

¼ tsp Sea Salt

1½ pounds Carrots, chopped

1 tbsp Coconut Cream

1½ cups Water

**Instructions:**

1. Pour the water into the Instant Pot. 2. Place the carrot inside the steaming basket then lower the basket into the pot. 3. Close the lid of the Instant Pot. To seal, turn the lid clockwise. 4. Select the "MANUAL" cooking mode after the chime. Using the "+" and "-" buttons, set the time to 4 minutes. Make sure to cook on HIGH pressure. 5. When the timer goes off, press the "KEEP WARM/CANCEL" button. 6. Turn the pressure handle to "Venting" to release the pressure quickly. 7. Open the lid carefully, keeping your hands away from the steam. 8. Take out the steaming basket and transfer the carrots to a food processor. 9. Add the rest of the ingredients. 10. Process until smooth. 11. Serve and enjoy!

**Per Serving:** Calories 75; Fat 1.64g; Sodium 246mg; Carbs 14.85g; Fiber 5.4g; Sugar 5.89g; Protein 1.52g

# Kohlrabi with Creamy Mushroom

**Prep Time: 15 minutes | Cook Time: 25 minutes | Servings: 4**

**Ingredients:**

¾ pound kohlrabi, trimmed and thinly sliced

3 tablespoons butter

½ pound mushrooms, sliced

½ cup scallions, chopped

1 garlic clove, minced

1 teaspoon sea salt

½ teaspoon ground black pepper

¼ teaspoon red pepper flakes

1½ cups double cream

**Instructions:**

1. Parboil kohlrabi in a large pot of salted water for 7 to 9 minutes. Drain and set aside. 2. Warm the butter over medium-high heat. Sauté the mushrooms, scallions, and garlic until tender and fragrant. 3. Season with salt, black pepper, and red pepper flakes. 4. Slowly stir in double cream, whisking continuously until the sauce has thickened, about 8 to 12 minutes. 5. Pour the mushroom sauce over the kohlrabi and serve warm.

**Per Serving:** Calories 293; Fat 26.34g; Sodium 708mg; Carbs 11.84g; Fiber 4.1g; Sugar 6.94g; Protein 6.04g

# Spicy Cabbage and Squash Kimchi

**Prep Time: 1 hour and 10 minutes | Cook time: 0 minutes | Servings: 6**

**Ingredients:**

3 tablespoons salt

1 pound napa cabbage, chopped

3 oz butternut squash, julienned

½ cup daikon radish

3 green onion stalks, chopped

1 tablespoon fish sauce

3 tablespoons chili flakes

3 garlic cloves, peeled and minced

1 tablespoon sesame oil

½–inchfresh ginger, peeled and grated

**Instructions:**

1. In a bowl, mix cabbage with salt, massage well for 10 minutes, cover, and set aside for 1 hour. 2. In a bowl, mix the chili flakes with fish sauce, garlic, sesame oil, ginger, and stir well. 3. Drain cabbage well, rinse under cold water, and transfer to a bowl. 4. Add squash, green onions, radish, and chili paste, and stir. 5. Leave in a dark and cold place for at least 2 days before serving.

**Per Serving:** Calories 53; Fat 3.03g; Sodium 3881mg; Carbs 6.63g; Fiber 2g; Sugar 0.97g; Protein 1.87g

# Cheese-Crusted Green Beans

## Prep Time: 10 minutes | Cook time: 10 minutes | Servings: 4

**Ingredients:**

⅔ cup Parmesan cheese, grated

1 egg

12 ounces green beans

Salt and ground black pepper, to taste

½ teaspoon garlic powder

¼ teaspoon paprika

**Instructions:**

1. In a bowl, mix Parmesan cheese with salt, pepper, garlic powder, and paprika. In another bowl, whisk egg with salt and pepper. 2. Coat the green beans in egg, and then in the Parmesan mixture. 3. Place green beans on a lined baking sheet, place in an oven at 400ºF for 10 minutes. 4. Serve hot.

Per Serving: Calories 128; Fat 7.51g; Sodium 331mg; Carbs 7.69g; Fiber 1.9g; Sugar 1.44g; Protein 8.27g

# Sautéed Cabbage, Pear, and Onion

## Prep Time: 10 minutes | Cook Time: 25 minutes | Servings: 4

**Ingredients:**

1 pound Cabbage, shredded

1 cup diced Onions

1 cup peeled and chopped Pears

1 tbsp Arrowroot

2 tbsp Water

1½ cups Chicken or Veggie Stock

1 tbsp Coconut Oil

½ tsp Sea Salt

¼ tsp Pepper

¼ tsp Cumin

**Instructions:**

1. Turn the Instant Pot on. Set it to "SAUTE" and add the coconut oil to it. 2. When melted, add the onions and pears and cook for about 6-7 minutes. 3. When softened, add the rest of the ingredients except the arrowroot and water. 4. Close the lid and turn clockwise to seal. Select the "MANUAL" cooking mode. Set the cooking time to 15 minutes. Cook on HIGH pressure. 5. When the timer goes off, press the "KEEP WARM/CANCEL" button. 6. Turn the handle to "Venting" for a quick pressure release, then open the lid carefully. 7. Whisk together the arrowroot and water and then whisk this mixture into the pot. 8. Set the Instant Pot to "SAUTE" again. 9. Cook for about 3 minutes until the sauce thickens. 10. Serve and enjoy!

Per Serving: Calories 134; Fat 3.73g; Sodium 326mg; Carbs 25.88g; Fiber 4.1g; Sugar 15.82g; Protein 2.16g

# Minty Snap Peas

**Prep Time: 15 minutes | Cook Time: 5 minutes | Servings: 4**

**Ingredients:**

¾ pound sugar snap peas, trimmed

1 tablespoon mint leaves, chopped.

3 green onions, chopped.

1 garlic clove, minced

2 teaspoons olive oil

Salt and black pepper to the taste.

**Instructions:**

1. Heat up a pan with the oil over medium high heat. 2. Add snap peas, salt, pepper, green onions, garlic and mint. 3. Stir everything, cook for 5 minutes, divide between plates and serve.

**Per Serving:** Calories 76; Fat 2.7g; Sodium 12mg; Carbs 10.83g; Fiber 3.4g; Sugar 6.08g; Protein 3.18g

# Potato and Carrot Salad

**Prep Time: 15 minutes | Cook Time: 10 minutes | Servings: 6**

**Ingredients:**

½ cup chopped Scallions

3 Celery Stalks, chopped

1 Large Carrot, peeled and chopped

½ Red Onion, sliced

4 Hardboiled Eggs, sliced, optional

1½ pounds Potatoes

⅓ cup Mayonnaise( or Avocado Oil Mayo)

½ tbsp Vinegar

½ tsp Sea Salt

⅓ tsp Cayenne Pepper

¼ tsp Black Pepper

2 cups Water

**Instructions:**

1. Wash the potatoes well, scrub them, and place inside the Instant Pot. Pour the water over them and put the lid on. Turn it clockwise to seal. 2. Select the "MANUAL" cooking mode. Set the cooking time to 10 minutes. Cook on HIGH pressure. 3. When the timer rings, turn the Instant Pot off by selecting "KEEP WARM/CANCEL". Turn the handle to "Venting" for a quick pressure release and open the lid carefully. Transfer the potatoes to a bowl and let them cool slightly. 4. When safe to handle, peel the potatoes and chop them. Season the potatoes with salt, cayenne, and black pepper. 5. Place the potatoes in a bowl along with the carrot, celery, onion, and scallions. In a bowl, whisk together the mayo and vinegar and sprinkle over the salad. If using eggs, slice them thinly and arrange on top. 6. Serve and enjoy!

**Per Serving:** Calories 271; Fat 16.22g; Sodium 290mg; Carbs 23.04g; Fiber 3.3g; Sugar 2.24g; Protein 8.76g

# Herbed Portobello Mushrooms

Prep Time: 10 minutes | Cook time: 10 minutes | Servings: 4

**Ingredients:**

12 ounces Portobello mushrooms, sliced
Salt and ground black pepper, to taste
½ teaspoon dried basil
2 tablespoons olive oil

½ teaspoon tarragon, dried
½ teaspoon dried rosemary
½ teaspoon dried thyme
2 tablespoons balsamic vinegar

**Instructions:**

1. In a bowl, mix the oil with vinegar, salt, pepper, rosemary, tarragon, basil, and thyme, and whisk.
2. Add mushroom slices, toss to coat well, place them on a preheated grill over medium–high heat, cook for 5 minutes on both sides, and serve.

Per Serving: Calories 324; Fat 7.63g; Sodium 14mg; Carbs 66.66g; Fiber 10g; Sugar 3.65g; Protein 8.46g

# Cauliflower, Sweet Potato and Peas Bowl

Prep Time: 10 minutes | Cook Time: 20 minutes | Servings: 8

**Ingredients:**

6 cups cauliflower florets
2 sweet potatoes, peeled and cubed
2 tomatoes, diced
2 cups peas
1 tsp minced garlic

1 cup chopped scallions
1 tbsp coconut oil
4 cups stock, veggie or chicken
Salt and Pepper, to taste

**Instructions:**

1. Turn the Instant Pot on and set it to "SAUTE". 2. Add the coconut oil to it. When the oil becomes melted, add the scallions. Cook for about 3-4 minutes. 3. Then, add the cauliflower, tomatoes, and stock. 4. Close the lid and turn clockwise to seal. Select the "MANUAL" cooking mode and set the cooking time to 6 minutes. Cook on HIGH pressure. 5. After the beep, press the "KEEP WARM/ CANCEL" button. 6. Turn the pressure handle to "Venting" to quickly release pressure and carefully open the lid. Stir in the remaining ingredients. 7. Close and seal the lid and hit "MANUAL" once again. 8. Cook for 10 more minutes. Do a quick pressure release again. 9. Open the lid and serve. Enjoy!

Per Serving: Calories 66; Fat 2.98g; Sodium 231mg; Carbs 6.84g; Fiber 2.4g; Sugar 3.07g; Protein 4.8g

# Easy Okra and Tomatoes with Crispy Bacon

## Prep Time: 20 minutes | Cook Time: 10 minutes | Servings: 6

**Ingredients:**

1 pound okra, sliced

1 yellow onion, chopped.

2 bacon slices, chopped.

1 small green bell peppers, chopped.

14 ounces canned stewed tomatoes, chopped.

2 celery stalks, chopped.

Salt and black pepper to the taste.

**Instructions:**

1. Heat up a pan over medium high heat; add bacon; stir, brown for a few minutes, transfer to paper towels and leave aside for now. 2. Heat up the pan again over medium heat; add okra, bell pepper, onion and celery; stir and cook for 2 minutes. 3. Add tomatoes, salt and pepper; stir and cook for 3 minutes. 4. Divide on plates, garnish with crispy bacon and serve

**Per Serving:** Calories 97; Fat 5.32g; Sodium 129mg; Carbs 10.73g; Fiber 4.2g; Sugar 4.36g; Protein 3.54g

# Spinach and Strawberry Salad with Cheese

## Prep Time: 10 minutes | Cook Time: 0 minutes | Servings: 4

**Ingredients:**

4 cups baby spinach

½ cup strawberries, hulled and sliced

1 cup avocado, pitted, peeled and sliced

2 tablespoons olive oil

½ lime, freshly squeezed

½ teaspoon kosher salt

White pepper, to taste

⅓ cup brie cheese, crumbled

2 tablespoons fresh basil leaves, chopped

**Instructions:**

1. Pat the spinach leaves dry and transfer them to a salad bowl. 2. Add the slices of strawberries and avocado. 3. Now, make the dressing by whisking olive oil, lime juice, salt and white pepper. Dress the salad and top with crumbled cheese. 4. Serve garnished with fresh basil leaves. Bon appétit!

**Per Serving:** Calories 200; Fat 17.9g; Sodium 442mg; Carbs 6.23g; Fiber 3.6g; Sugar 1.44g; Protein 5.87g

# Chard and Cashews Side Dish

## Prep Time: 20 minutes | Cook Time: 11 minutes | Servings: 2

**Ingredients:**

½ cup cashews; chopped

1 bunch chard; cut into thin strips

A pinch of sea salt

Black pepper to the taste

1 tbsp. coconut oil

**Instructions:**

1. Heat up a pan with the oil over medium heat, add chard and cashews, stir and cook for 10 minutes. 2. Add a pinch of salt and pepper to the taste, stir; cook for 1 minute more, take off heat, transfer to plates and serve as a side dish.

Per Serving: Calories 457; Fat 40.78g; Sodium 190mg; Carbs 21.52g; Fiber 2.3g; Sugar 6.97g; Protein 8.21g

# Zucchini and Parsley Mash

## Prep Time: 10 minutes | Cook Time: 10 minutes | Servings: 4

**Ingredients:**

4 zucchini, cut in half

¼ cup parsley, chopped

1 tbsp lemon juice

1 tbsp olive oil

2 garlic cloves

1 tsp cumin

2½ tbsp tahini

Pepper

Salt

**Instructions:**

1. Place zucchini on hot grill and season with pepper and salt. 2. Grilled zucchini for 10 minutes. 3. Add grilled zucchini, parsley, cumin, tahini, lemon juice, olive oil, garlic, pepper and salt in a blender and blend until smooth. 4. Pour zucchini mixture in a bowl and sprinkle with paprika. 5. Serve and enjoy.

Per Serving: Calories 130; Fat 9.23g; Sodium 31mg; Carbs 10.38g; Fiber 3.2g; Sugar 5.67g; Protein 4.5g

# Grilled Cajun Veggies

## Prep Time: 10 minutes | Cook Time: 15 minutes | Servings: 4

**Ingredients:**

4 bell peppers, diced

2 eggplants, diced

2 tbsp olive oil

2 cups mushrooms, sliced

1 tsp Cajun seasoning

¼ tsp pepper

1 tsp salt

**Instructions:**

1. Add all vegetables in a baking dish and drizzle with olive oil and season with seasoning, pepper and salt. 2. Cook at 392°F for 15-20 minutes. 3. Serve and enjoy.

**Per Serving:** Calories 150; Fat 7.35g; Sodium 643mg; Carbs 21.15g; Fiber 9.1g; Sugar 12.25g; Protein 3.77g

# Easy Steamed Potatoes

## Prep Time: 7 minutes | Cook Time: 8 minutes | Servings: 8

**Ingredients:**

3 pounds Potatoes, peeled and quartered

1 tsp Cayenne Pepper

1 tsp Sea Salt

½ tsp Black Pepper

Water, as needed

**Instructions:**

1. Place the potatoes inside the Instant Pot. 2. Add enough water to cover them. 3. Close the lid and turn clockwise to seal. 4. Choose the "MANUAL" mode and then set the cooking time to 8 minutes. Cook on HIGH pressure. 5. When the timer goes off, press the "KEEP WARM/CANCEL" button. 6. Turn the pressure handle to "Venting" to do a quick pressure release. 7. Drain the potatoes and place them in a bowl. 8. Chop them if you want to. 9. Sprinkle with the seasonings and serve. 10. Enjoy!

**Per Serving:** Calories 132; Fat 0.2g; Sodium 301mg; Carbs 29.96g; Fiber 3.9g; Sugar 1.35g; Protein 3.48g

# Avocado Green Beans Salad

## Prep Time: 10 minutes | Cook time: 5 minutes | Servings: 6

**Ingredients:**

1 lb fresh green beans, trimmed

¼ cup green onion, chopped

3 avocado, peel and mashed

4 tbsp olive oil

¼ tsp pepper

¼ tsp salt

**Instructions:**

1. Heat olive oil in pan over medium high heat. 2. Add green beans in pan and sauté for 4 minutes. 3. Season beans with pepper and salt and set aside. 4. In a mixing bowl, add green beans, avocado, and green onion and mix well. 5. Serve and enjoy.

**Per Serving:** Calories 259; Fat 24.1g; Sodium 106mg; Carbs 12.19g; Fiber 8.3g; Sugar 1.47g; Protein 2.92g

# Delicious Asparagus Mash

## Prep Time: 10 minutes | Cook time: 10 minutes | Servings: 2

**Ingredients:**

10 asparagus spears, trimmed and chopped

1 tsp lemon juice

2 tbsp coconut cream

1 small onion, diced

2 tbsp fresh parsley, chopped

1 tbsp olive oil

Pepper

Salt

**Instructions:**

1. Sauté onion in pan over medium heat until onion is softened. 2. Blanch chopped asparagus in boiling water for 2 minutes and drain well. 3. Add sautéed onion, lemon juice, parsley, coconut cream, asparagus, pepper, and salt into the blender and blend until smooth. 4. Serve and enjoy.

**Per Serving:** Calories 138; Fat 12.09g; Sodium 6mg; Carbs 7.49g; Fiber 1.8g; Sugar 3.06g; Protein 1.89g

# Roasted Spiced Summer Squash

## Prep Time: 10 minutes | Cook time: 60 minutes | Servings: 3

**Ingredients:**

2 lbs summer squash, cut into 1-inch pieces

¼ tsp garlic powder

3 tbsp olive oil

1 tbsp lemon juice

¼ tsp paprika

Pepper

Salt

**Instructions:**

1. Preheat the oven to 400°F. 2. Place squash pieces onto a baking tray and drizzle with olive oil. 3. Season with garlic powder, paprika, pepper, and salt. 4. Drizzle with lemon juice and bake in oven for 50-60 minutes. 5. Serve and enjoy.

**Per Serving:** Calories 249; Fat 13.87g; Sodium 11mg; Carbs 33.58g; Fiber 4.9g; Sugar 0.92g; Protein 2.81g

# Easy Spinach Omelet

## Prep Time: 10 minutes | Cook time: 5 minutes | Servings: 1

**Ingredients:**

2 eggs

½ cup baby spinach

1 tsp olive oil

Pepper

Salt

**Instructions:**

1. Add eggs, spinach, pepper, and salt in the blender and blend until well combined. Heat the olive oil in a pan over medium heat. 2. Pour egg mixture into a hot pan and cook for 2-3 minutes then flip to other side and cook for 2 minutes more. 3. Serve and enjoy.

**Per Serving:** Calories 320; Fat 23.93g; Sodium 219mg; Carbs 6.83g; Fiber 1g; Sugar 3.66g; Protein 19.26g

# Chinese-Style Green Bean Stir Fry

## Prep Time: 15 minutes | Cook Time: 30 minutes | Servings: 12

### Ingredients:

1 cup vegetable oil

13 pounds fresh green beans, trimmed

5 tablespoons minced garlic

5 tablespoons minced fresh ginger root

2 tablespoons kosher salt

1 tablespoon coarsely ground black pepper

2 (8 ounce) bottles black bean sauce

### Instructions:

1. In a big wok, on medium-high heat, heat oil. Mix in green beans, cook for 1-2 minutes, mixing often. 2. Blend in ginger and garlic, cook for 3-4 minutes, mixing often. 3. Season with pepper and salt and mix in black bean sauce. 4. Keep cooking till green beans become tender.

Per Serving: Calories 276; Fat 20.46g; Sodium 1173mg; Carbs 22.84g; Fiber 9.5g; Sugar 3.91g; Protein 5.77g

# Creamy Cauliflower Mash

## Prep Time: 10 minutes | Cook time: 10 minutes | Servings: 2

### Ingredients:

¼ cup sour cream

1 small cauliflower head, separated into florets

Salt and ground black pepper, to taste

2 tablespoons feta cheese, crumbled

2 tablespoons black olives, pitted and sliced

### Instructions:

1. Put water in a saucepan, add some salt, bring to a boil over medium heat, add the florets, cook for 10 minutes, take off heat, and drain. 2. Return cauliflower to the saucepan, add salt, black pepper, and sour cream, and blend using an immersion blender. 3. Add black olives and feta cheese, stir, and serve.

Per Serving: Calories 135; Fat 7.6g; Sodium 375mg; Carbs 12.61g; Fiber 3.3g; Sugar 4.86g; Protein 6.57g

# Chapter 3 Poultry Recipes

# Chicken and Cucumber Salad

## Prep Time: 20 minutes | Cook Time: 15 minutes | Servings: 6

### Ingredients

2 chicken breasts

2 medium-sized cucumbers, sliced

½ teaspoon coarse salt

¼ teaspoon ground black pepper

¼ teaspoon chili pepper flakes

**For the Dressing:**

2 garlic cloves, minced

2 large egg yolks

1 tablespoon fresh lime juice

½ teaspoon dried oregano

⅓ teaspoon dried basil

2 romaine hearts, leaves separated

¼ cup Parmesan, finely grated

1 teaspoon mustard

¼ cup olive oil

### Instructions:

1. Firstly, grill the chicken breast until done; cut them into cubes. 2. Toss the cucumbers and chicken with the salt, black pepper, chili pepper, oregano, and basil. Place the romaine leaves into a salad bowl. 3. Now, add the cucumber and chicken mixture. Prepare the dressing by whisking all the dressing ingredients. 4. Dress the salad; scatter parmesan over the top, serve and enjoy!

**Per Serving:** Calories 281; Fat 19.66g; Sodium 306mg; Carbs 2.5g; Fiber 0.2g; Sugar 0.27g; Protein 22.57g

# Cheese Spinach Stuffed Chicken

## Prep Time: 15 minutes | Cook Time: 30 minutes | Servings: 6

### Ingredients:

4 ounces cream cheese

3 ounces mozzarella slices

10 ounces spinach

⅓ cup shredded mozzarella

1 tbsp olive oil

1 cup tomato basil sauce

3 whole chicken breasts

### Instructions:

1. Preheat your oven to 400°F. Combine the cream cheese, mozzarella, and spinach in the microwave. 2. Cut the chicken with the knife a couple of times horizontally. Stuff with the filling. Brush the top with olive oil. Place on a lined baking dish and in the oven. Bake in the oven for 25 minutes. 3. Pour the sauce over and top with mozzarella. Return to oven and cook for 5 minutes.

**Per Serving:** Calories 435; Fat 24.56g; Sodium 955mg; Carbs 11.91g; Fiber 3.8g; Sugar 5.89g; Protein 39.18g

# Turkey Patties with Cucumber Salsa

## Prep Time: 30 minutes | Cook Time: 6 minutes | Servings: 4

### Ingredients:

2 spring onions, thinly sliced
1 pound ground turkey
1 egg
2 garlic cloves, minced
1 tbsp chopped herbs
1 small chili pepper, deseeded and diced
2 tbsp ghee
Cucumber Salsa

1 tbsp apple cider vinegar
1 tbsp chopped dill
1 garlic clove, minced
2 cucumbers, grated
1 cup sour cream
1 jalapeño pepper, minced
2 tbsp olive oil

### Instructions:

1. Place all turkey ingredients, except the ghee, in a bowl. Mix to combine. Make patties out of the mixture. Melt the ghee in a skillet over medium heat. Cook the patties for 3 minutes on each side. 2. Place all salsa ingredients in a bowl and mix to combine. Serve the patties topped with salsa.
Per Serving:  Calories 756; Fat 66.21g; Sodium 130mg; Carbs 11.97g; Fiber 2g; Sugar 3.73g; Protein 27.72g

# Grilled Juicy Chicken

## Prep Time: 15 minutes | Cook Time: 15 minutes | Servings: 4

### Ingredients:

½ cup grated onion (about 1 medium)
¼ cup lemon or lime juice
2 tablespoons extra-virgin olive oil
2 tablespoons garam masala

1 teaspoon salt
1-1¼ pounds boneless, skinless chicken breast

### Instructions:

1. In a bowl, combine salt, onion, garam masala, oil, and lemon or lime juice until blended. 2. In a one-gallon sealable plastic bag or a shallow dish; put chicken and the marinade. Chill for at least an hour and up to 12hrs. Take the chicken out of the marinade then pat dry. 3. Set the grill on medium-high heat or place a rack in the top third of the oven then preheat the broiler. 4. For the grill: grease the grill rack then place the chicken. Grill for 4-8mins on each side, turning once, until an inserted instant-read thermometer in the thickest part reads 165°F. 5. For the broiler: Line foil on a baking sheet or broiler pan then grease with cooking spray. Put the chicken over the foil; broil for 10-15mins in total until an inserted instant-read thermometer in the thickest part reads 165°F. Turn at least one time, watching carefully.
Per Serving: Calories 235; Fat 9.5g; Sodium 947mg; Carbs 26.57g; Fiber 2.1g; Sugar 7g; Protein 10.84g

# Crispy Chicken Legs

## Prep Time: 10 minutes | Cook Time: 45 minutes | Servings: 4

**Ingredients:**

1 tablespoon butter

4 chicken legs

¼ teaspoon ground black pepper or to taste

Salt, to your liking

1 teaspoon bouillon powder

1 teaspoon dried rosemary

1 teaspoon paprika

1 teaspoon dried basil

**Instructions:**

1. Put the oven on at 420°F. Line a baking sheet with parchment paper. 2. Air-dry the chicken legs and then put the butter on them. Sprinkle the pepper, salt, bouillon powder, rosemary, paprika and basil on the legs. 3. Put the chicken legs on the baking sheet. 4. Bake the chicken legs for about 45 minutes. By this time the shin should be crispy. Serve with a spicy sauce.

Per Serving: Calories 349; Fat 14.17g; Sodium 278mg; Carbs 1.17g; Fiber 0.4g; Sugar 0.25g; Protein 51.05g

# Chicken and Veggie Stew

## Prep Time: 15 minutes | Cook Time: 1 hour | Servings: 6

**Ingredients:**

2 tablespoons tallow, room temperature

2 medium-sized shallots, finely chopped

2 garlic cloves, sliced

1 quart chicken broth

1 sprig rosemary

1 teaspoon dried marjoram

1 pound chicken drumsticks

1 celery, chopped

½ pound carrots, chopped

1 bell pepper, chopped

1 poblano pepper, chopped

2 ripe tomatoes, chopped

1 teaspoon salt

½ teaspoon ground black pepper

½ teaspoon smoked paprika

**Instructions:**

1. Melt the tallow in a large heavy pot that is preheated over a moderate flame. Sweat the shallots and garlic until aromatic and just tender. 2. Now, turn the heat to medium-high. Stir in the chicken broth, rosemary, marjoram, and chicken drumsticks; bring to a boil. 3. Add the remaining ingredients and reduce the heat to medium-low. Simmer, covered, for 50 minutes. 4. Discard the bones and chop the chicken into small chunks. Serve hot!

Per Serving: Calories 197; Fat 11.5g; Sodium 511mg; Carbs 8.44g; Fiber 2.3g; Sugar 4.16g; Protein 15.01g

# Chicken and Rutabaga Soup

**Ingredients:**

1 pound chicken thighs

½ cup rutabaga, cubed

2 carrots, peeled

2 celery stalks

½ cup leek, chopped

¼ teaspoon garlic, granulated

¼ teaspoon ground cloves

½ cup taro leaves, roughly chopped

1 tablespoon fresh parsley, chopped

Salt and black pepper, to taste

1 cup chicken consommé, canned

3 cups water

1 teaspoon cayenne pepper

**Instructions:**

1. Add all of the above ingredients, except forcayenne pepper, to a large-sized stock pot. Bring to a rapid boil over high heat. 2. Now, turn the heat to medium-low. Let it simmer, partially covered, an additional 35 minutes or until the chicken is pinkish-brown. 3. Next, discard the chicken and vegetables. Add cayenne pepper to the broth; allow it to simmer an additional 8 minutes. 4. When the chicken thighs are cool enough to handle, cut off the meat from bones. Afterwards, add the meat back to the soup and serve warm.

Per Serving: Calories 551; Fat 25.57g; Sodium 351mg; Carbs 8.26g; Fiber 2.1g; Sugar 3.74g; Protein 68.35g

# Chili Chicken Wings

**Ingredients:**

3 tablespoons olive oil

3 cloves garlic, pressed

2 teaspoons chili powder

1 teaspoon garlic powder

Salt and ground black pepper to taste

10 chicken wings

**Instructions:**

1. Prepare the oven by preheating to 375°F. 2. Mix the pepper, salt, garlic powder, chili powder, garlic, and olive oil in a large resealable bag; close and shake to mix. Put in the chicken wings; close again and shake to coat. Transfer chicken wings to a baking sheet and arrange them. 3. Place the chicken wings in the preheated oven and cook for 1 hour, or until cooked through and crisp.

Per Serving: Calories 390; Fat 25.85g; Sodium 199mg; Carbs 6.09g; Fiber 1.5g; Sugar 1.42g; Protein 33.21g

# Roasted Thyme Chicken Thighs

Prep Time: 15 minutes | Cook Time: 17 minutes | Servings: 2

**Ingredients:**

2 boneless, skinless chicken thighs (about 8 ounces)

¼ teaspoon kosher salt

¼ teaspoon dried thyme

¼ teaspoon ground pepper

**Instructions:**

1. Preheat the oven to 400°F. Line foil or parchment onto a baking sheet. 2. Put the chicken onto the baking sheet. Drizzle around the chicken with pepper, salt, and thyme. Roast, turning once, for about 15 to 17 minutes until the chicken is cooked through and the internal temperature reaches 165°F.

Per Serving: Calories 138; Fat 2.98g; Sodium 342mg; Carbs 0.56g; Fiber 0.1g; Sugar 0.29g; Protein 25.63g

# Cilantro Chicken with Mayo-Avocado Sauce

Prep Time: 10 minutes | Cook Time: 20 minutes | Servings: 4

**Ingredients**

For the Sauce:

1 avocado, pitted

½ cup mayonnaise

Salt to taste

For the Chicken:

3 tbsp ghee

4 chicken breasts

Pink salt and black pepper to taste

1 cup chopped cilantro leaves

½ cup chicken broth

**Instructions:**

1. Spoon the avocado, mayonnaise, and salt into a small food processor and puree until smooth sauce is derived. Adjust taste with salt as desired. 2. Pour sauce into a jar and refrigerate while you make the chicken. 3. Melt ghee in a large skillet, season chicken with salt and black pepper and fry for 4 minutes on each side to golden brown. Remove chicken to a plate. 4. Pour the broth in the same skillet and add the cilantro. Bring to simmer covered for 3 minutes and add the chicken. 5. Cover and cook on low heat for 5 minutes until liquid has reduced and chicken is fragrant. 6. Dish chicken only into serving plates and spoon the mayo-avocado sauce over.

Per Serving: Calories 729; Fat 45.85g; Sodium 544mg; Carbs 6.65g; Fiber 4g; Sugar 1.2g; Protein 70.05g

# Tahini Chicken Skewers

**Prep Time: 2 hours | Cook Time: 10 minutes | Servings: 4**

**Ingredients:**

For the Skewers:

3 tbsp soy sauce

1 tbsp ginger-garlic paste

2 tbsp swerve brown sugar

For the Dressing:

½ cup tahini

½ tsp garlic powder

Chili pepper to taste

2 tbsp olive oil

3 chicken breasts, cut into cubes

Pink salt to taste

¼ cup warm water

**Instructions:**

1. In a bowl, whisk the soy sauce, ginger-garlic paste, brown sugar, chili pepper, and olive oil. 2. Put the chicken in a zipper bag, pour the marinade over, seal and shake for an even coat. Marinate in the fridge for 2 hours. 3. Preheat a grill to 400ºF and thread the chicken on skewers. Cook for 10 minutes in total with three to four turnings to be golden brown. Plate them. Mix the tahini, garlic powder, salt, and warm water in a bowl. Pour into serving jars. 4. Serve the chicken skewers and tahini dressing with cauli fried rice.

**Per Serving:** Calories 649; Fat 45.17g; Sodium 353mg; Carbs 9.89g; Fiber 3.1g; Sugar 2.49g; Protein 51.39g

# Simple Marinated Chicken

**Prep Time: 15 minutes | Cook Time: 25 minutes | Servings: 4**

**Ingredients:**

1 egg

1 cup vegetable oil

2 cups cider vinegar

3 tablespoons salt

1 tablespoon poultry seasoning

1 teaspoon ground black pepper

4 chicken thighs

**Instructions:**

1. Crack and whisk an egg in a medium bowl until beaten. Slowly whisk in the oil until it blends completely. 2. Mix in ground black pepper, poultry seasoning, salt, and vinegar. Save some sauce aside for basting later on. 3. Coat the chicken with the sauce in a shallow baking dish. Cover and marinate the chicken in the refrigerator for 24 hours. Roast for 20-25 minutes.

**Per Serving:** Calories 544; Fat 57.02g; Sodium 5264mg; Carbs 2.55g; Fiber 0.3g; Sugar 0.67g; Protein 2.42g

# Healthy Chicken and Avocado Salad

Prep Time: 20 minutes | Cook Time: 10 minutes | Servings: 4

**Ingredients:**

2 chicken breasts

⅓ teaspoon crushed red pepper flakes

½ teaspoon sea salt

¼ teaspoon dried thyme, or to taste

1 large pitted and sliced avocado

2 egg yolks

1 tablespoon Worcestershire sauce

⅓ cup olive oil

1 tablespoon lime juice

½ teaspoon mustard powder

⅓ teaspoon sea salt

**Instructions:**

1. Put your grill on high. Season the chicken breasts with pepper, salt and thyme. Cook each side of the chicken for 3 – 5 minutes until browned. 2. Cut the grilled chicken into strips. 3. Put the sliced avocado onto 4 plates. 4. Make the dressing. Combine the egg yolks, Worcestershire sauce, olive oil, lime juice, mustard powder and sea salt. 5. Put the chicken strips on top of the avocado and then pour the dressing over them. Enjoy!

Per Serving: Calories 520; Fat 40.89g; Sodium 632mg; Carbs 5.8g; Fiber 3.4g; Sugar 0.89g; Protein 32.63g

# Lemon Baked Whole Chicken

Prep Time: 15 minutes | Cook Time: 3 hours | Servings: 4

**Ingredients:**

1 (4 pound) whole chicken

2 tablespoons salt

1 lemon, halved

1 tablespoon paprika

1 cup water

**Instructions:**

1. Set the oven to 300°F for preheating. 2. Rub the salt all over the inner and outer portion of the chicken. Squeeze the lemon juice from the lemon halves all over the outer parts of the chicken, and then rub it with paprika. 3. After using the squeezed lemon halves, place them inside the cavity of the chicken. 4. Position the chicken in a 9x13-inches baking dish that is lightly greased. To prevent the chicken from drying, pour in a small amount of water. 5. Let it bake inside the preheated oven for 3 hours while basting the chicken with water if necessary.

Per Serving: Calories 239; Fat 5.89g; Sodium 3647mg; Carbs 1.75g; Fiber 0.6g; Sugar 0.48g; Protein 42.77g

# Bacon Wrapped Chicken

## Prep Time: 15 minutes | Cook Time: 30 minutes | Servings: 6

**Ingredients:**

6 chicken breast halves, skinless, boneless and pounded flat

salt and ground black pepper to taste

6 tablespoons prepared basil pesto

6 slices bacon

½ cup vegetable oil

**Instructions:**

1. Heat the oven to 400°. 2. Lay the chicken breast flat and season with salt and pepper. Spread pesto sauce on the chicken, wrap chicken breast with bacon, secure roll with some toothpicks. Put the rolled chicken breast in 9x9 inch dish. Do the same with the rest of the chicken breasts. Pour vegetable oil on the chicken. 3. Bake for 30 minutes until the bacon turns crisp and the meat is not pink inside. An instant read thermometer poked in center of one roll should read 160°F or higher.

**Per Serving:** Calories 769; Fat 55.23g; Sodium 306mg; Carbs 1g; Fiber 0.2g; Sugar 0.61g; Protein 63.96g

# Lemon-Garlic Chicken with Potatoes

## Prep Time: 15 minutes | Cook Time: 27 minutes | Servings: 4

**Ingredients:**

4 teaspoons canola oil or extra-virgin olive oil, divided

1 teaspoon crushed dried thyme, divided

½ teaspoon kosher salt or ¼ teaspoon regular salt

¼ teaspoon freshly ground black pepper

1 pound fingerling potatoes, halved

lengthwise, or tiny new red or white potatoes, halved

4 small skinless, boneless chicken breast halves (1 to 1¼ pounds total)

2 cloves garlic, minced

1 lemon, thinly sliced

**Instructions:**

1. On medium heat, heat 2tsp oil in a very big pan; mix in pepper, salt, and half teaspoon thyme. Toss in potatoes to coat; cover. Cook for 12minutes, mixing two times. 2. Mix and push the potatoes in one corner of the pan; put in 2tsp oil. Place the chicken breast halves on the other corner of the pan; cook for 5mins without cover. 3. Flip the chicken breasts and slather garlic on top; add the remaining half teaspoon of thyme. Top chicken with slices of lemon; cover. Cook for another 7-10 minutes until the potatoes are tender and the chicken reaches 170°F and not pink.

**Per Serving:** Calories 269; Fat 7.64g; Sodium 349mg; Carbs 21.18g; Fiber 2.6g; Sugar 1.2g; Protein 27.99g

# Spiced Chicken with Lemony Brussels Sprouts

Prep Time: 15 minutes | Cook Time: 25 minutes | Servings: 4

**Ingredients:**

1 pound Brussels sprouts, trimmed and halved (or quartered if large)

4 small shallots, quartered

1 lemon, sliced

3 tablespoons extra-virgin olive oil, divided

¾ teaspoon salt, divided

½ teaspoon ground pepper, divided

2 cloves garlic, minced

1 tablespoon smoked paprika, sweet or hot

1 teaspoon dried thyme

4 large or 8 small bone-in chicken thighs (about 2½ pounds), skin removed

**Instructions:**

1. In lower third of oven, position the rack; preheat to 450°F. 2. On a large rimmed baking sheet, combine lemon, shallots and Brussels sprouts together with ¼ teaspoon each salt and pepper and 2 tablespoons of olive oil. 3. Mash garlic and the remaining half a teaspoon salt, using the side of a chef's knife in order to form a paste. In a small bowl, combine the remaining 1 tablespoon oil, thyme, garlic paste, paprika, and ¼ teaspoon pepper. Rub the paste all over chicken. Nestle the chicken into Brussels sprouts. 4. Roast on the lower rack for around 20 to 25 minutes till the Brussels sprouts are softened and an instant-read thermometer inserted into the thickest part of the chicken without touching bone measures 165°F.

Per Serving: Calories 352; Fat 21.15g; Sodium 1027mg; Carbs 13.71g; Fiber 5.2g; Sugar 3.59g; Protein 29.01g

# Tasty Turkey Legs

Prep Time: 15 minutes | Cook Time: 7-8 hours | Servings: 6

**Ingredients:**

6 turkey legs

3 teaspoons poultry seasoning, divided

salt and ground black pepper to taste

6 12x16-inch squares of aluminum foil

**Instructions:**

1. Rinse turkey legs, and shake off extra liquid. Scatter every turkey leg with approximately ½ teaspoon of the poultry seasoning, black pepper and salt to taste. 2. Securely wrap leg with aluminum foil. Redo with the rest of legs into a slow cooker, put wrapped legs of turkey without any other ingredients or liquids. 3. Turn cooker to Low, and cook for 7 to 8 hours till meat is really soft.

Per Serving: Calories 1180; Fat 54.91g; Sodium 605mg; Carbs 1.2g; Fiber 0.2g; Sugar 0.4g; Protein 159.67g

# Grilled Lime Chicken Wings

Prep Time: 2 hours and 10 minutes | Cook time: 15 minutes | Servings: 5

**Ingredients:**

2 pounds wings

Juice from 1 lime

½ cup fresh cilantro, chopped

2 garlic cloves, peeled and minced

1 jalapeño pepper, chopped

3 tablespoons coconut oil

Salt and ground black pepper, to taste

Lime wedges, for serving

Mayonnaise, for serving

**Instructions:**

1. In a bowl, mix lime juice with cilantro, garlic, jalapeño, coconut oil, salt, and pepper, and whisk.
2. Add chicken wings, toss to coat, and keep in the refrigerator for 2 hours. 3. Place chicken wings on a preheated grill pan over medium–high heat, and cook for 7 minutes on each side. 4. Serve the chicken wings with mayonnaise and lime wedges.

**Per Serving:** Calories 173; Fat 9.8g; Sodium 10mg; Carbs 11.46g; Fiber 0.4g; Sugar 1.24g; Protein 13.15g

# Spiced Chicken with Chorizo Sausage

Prep Time: 15 minutes | Cook Time: 3-4 hours | Servings: 6

**Ingredients:**

4 skinless, boneless chicken breast halves

1 onion, chopped

1 (15 ounce) can tomato sauce

1 (7 ounce) can chipotle chile peppers in adobo sauce, chopped and seeded

2 fresh jalapeno peppers, seeded and chopped

2 cloves garlic, minced

1 teaspoon ground oregano

1 teaspoon ground cumin

1 teaspoon chili powder

¼ teaspoon red pepper flakes

¾ (1 pound) chorizo sausage

**Instructions:**

1. In a slow cooker, combine chipotle chile pepper, tomato sauce, onion, chicken with red pepper flakes, chili powder, cumin, oregano, garlic, jalapeno peppers, and adobo sauce. 2. Set the cooker to Low, cook for 2-3 hours until chicken is not pink inside anymore. Take chicken out of slow cooker, use two forks to shred then bring back to the slow cooker. 3. Heat a big skillet on medium-high heat, add chorizo sausage; stir and cook about 5-10 minutes until crumbly and brown. Drain then throw away grease. Put chorizo in the chicken mixture and stir. 4. Choose Low setting on the slow cooker, cook about ¾ hour - 1 hour.

**Per Serving:** Calories 392; Fat 15.44g; Sodium 686mg; Carbs 11.74g; Fiber 3.9g; Sugar 3.33g; Protein 52.5g

# Herbed Garlic Chicken

**Prep Time: 15 minutes | Cook Time: 15 minutes | Servings: 6**

## Ingredients:

6 boneless chicken breast halves (about 1½ pounds total)

¼ cup olive oil

6 cloves garlic, minced

1 tablespoon lemon peel, finely shredded

2 teaspoons snipped fresh thyme

1 teaspoon snipped fresh rosemary

¼ teaspoon crushed red pepper

¼ teaspoon salt

⅛ teaspoon ground black pepper

Fresh thyme sprigs (optional)

Lemon wedges (optional)

## Instructions:

1. Transfer the chicken to a resealable plastic bag and set in a shallow bowl. For the marinade, mix oil, crushed red pepper, garlic, black pepper, lemon peel, rosemary, salt and thyme in a small bowl. Spread the marinade atop chicken. Seal the bag and flip to coat the chicken. Place in a fridge to marinate for about 2 to 4 hours and turn the bag often. 2. Drain the chicken and get rid of the marinade. Transfer the chicken onto the rack of an uncovered grill directly atop medium coals. Let it grill for about 12 to 15 minutes or until no pink color of chicken remains, flipping once halfway through grilling (165°F). 3. Stud with lemon wedges and fresh thyme sprigs if desired.

**Per Serving:** Calories 223; Fat 12.02g; Sodium 149mg; Carbs 1.89g; Fiber 0.3g; Sugar 0.33g; Protein 25.79g

# Apple & Cranberry Stuffed Pork Chops

## Prep Time: 15 minutes | Cook Time: 1 hour | Servings: 3

**Ingredients:**

1 tablespoon olive oil

½ onion, chopped

1 large Granny Smith apple - peeled, cored and diced

2 tablespoons balsamic vinegar

½ cup dried cranberries

Salt and pepper to taste

2 (6 ounce) boneless pork chops

1 tablespoon olive oil

**Instructions:**

1. In a skillet over medium heat, heat 1 tablespoon olive oil. Mix in apple and onion; cook while stirring for 5 minutes. Mix in balsamic vinegar and cranberries and keep cooking until the onions and apple are tender, about 5 more minutes. Sprinkle with pepper and salt to season; on a plate, scrape the mixture and refrigerate to cold. 2. Set oven to 350°F to preheat. In a small baking dish, lightly grease. 3. Use a sharp, thin bladed knife to cut a large pocket into the pork chops. In the pork chops, stuff the cooled apple mixture and use toothpicks to secure (if needed). In a large skillet, heat leftover 1 tablespoon of olive oil over medium-high heat. Sprinkle the pork chops with pepper and salt to taste, and put into the hot skillet. Cook for 3 minutes per side until brown, then place into a baking dish. Add the leftover apple mixture on top and use aluminum foil to cover the baking dish. 4. Bake in prepared oven for about 40 minutes depending on the thick of pork chops, until the center of the pork remains no pink. 5. Bake without a cover for 10 more minutes until the edges of apple mixture have browned.

Per Serving: Calories 322; Fat 13.44g; Sodium 66mg; Carbs 19.99g; Fiber 2.5g; Sugar 14.73g; Protein 28.5g

# Chapter 4 Beef, Pork, and Lamb Recipes

# Pork and Veggie Stew

## Prep Time: 10 minutes | Cook Time: 8 hours | Servings: 8

### Ingredients:

2 lbs. pork loin; cubed and marinated in some beer in the fridge for 1 day

1 tbsp. coconut oil

3 garlic cloves; minced

1 cup arrowroot flour

6 carrots; chopped

Black pepper to the taste

A pinch of sea salt

2 yellow onions; chopped

1 small cabbage head; finely chopped

5 small sweet potatoes; chopped

30 oz. canned tomatoes; chopped

3 cups beef stock

### Instructions:

1. In a bowl mix arrowroot flour with marinated pork cubes and rub them well. 2. Heat up a pan with the oil over medium high heat, add pork cubes, brown them on all sides and transfer to your slow cooker. 3. Add garlic, carrots, a pinch of salt, black pepper, onion, cabbage, sweet potatoes, tomatoes and stock, stir; cover pot and cook your stew on Low for 8 hours. Uncover pot, stir stew again, divide into bowls and serve.

Per Serving: Calories 381; Fat 7.7g; Sodium 431mg; Carbs 42.32g; Fiber 7.4g; Sugar 14.48g; Protein 36.47g

# Beef and Plantains Stew

## Prep Time: 10 minutes | Cook Time: 8 hours | Servings: 4

### Ingredients:

2½ lbs. beef chuck; cubed

3 cups collard greens

3 cups water

5 green plantains; peeled and cubed

3 tbsp. allspice

¼ cup garlic powder

⅓ cup sweet paprika

1 tsp. cayenne pepper

1 tsp. chili powder

### Instructions:

1. In your slow cooker, mix beef with greens, plantains, water, allspice, garlic powder, paprika, cayenne and chili powder, stir well, cover and cook on Low for 8 hours. 2. Keep stirring from time to time. Divide into bowls and serve.

Per Serving: Calories 656; Fat 18.45g; Sodium 295mg; Carbs 70.19g; Fiber 10.3g; Sugar 25.2g; Protein 63.63g

# Mixed Meat and Veggie Stew

## Prep Time: 10 minutes | Cook time: 4 hours | Servings: 8

**Ingredients:**

2 leeks, chopped

2 yellow onions, chopped

1 carrot, chopped

3 garlic cloves, minced

1 and ½ teaspoons thyme, chopped

3 cups veggie stock

1 tablespoon lemon juice

3 tablespoons parsley, chopped

Pinch of salt and black pepper

1 pound beef chuck, cubed

1 pound pork butt, cubed

1 pound lamb shoulder, cubed

3 sweet potatoes, cubed

1 tablespoon coconut oil, melted

**Instructions:**

1. In a Dutch oven, mix all the ingredients, toss, cover, and bake in the oven at 350°F for 4 hours. 2. Divide into bowls and serve. 3. Enjoy!

**Per Serving:** Calories 497; Fat 25.78g; Sodium 443mg; Carbs 19.33g; Fiber 6.8g; Sugar 3.11g; Protein 47.64g

# Herbed Pork Loin Roast with Bacon

## Prep Time: 15 minutes | Cook Time: 2 hours | Servings: 16

**Ingredients:**

1 (5 pound) pork loin roast

1 tablespoon olive oil

1 pound sliced bacon

3 cups chicken stock

1 tablespoon dried rosemary

1 tablespoon dried thyme

6 fresh basil leaves

6 fresh sage leaves

4 cloves garlic, chopped

8 fresh pearl onions, peeled

**Instructions:**

1. Turn the oven to 300°F to preheat. 2. In a roasting pan, brush pork loin with olive oil. Drape slices of bacon on top. Mix the thyme, chicken stock, rosemary, sage, basil and garlic. Put above the roast. 3. Arrange onions around the sides. Cover with a lid or aluminum oil. 4. Place for an hour and 30 minutes to bake. Remove the cover or foil, bake for another half an hour, or until the bacon is browned. Cook at least 145°F.

**Per Serving:** Calories 478; Fat 21.64g; Sodium 305mg; Carbs 13.08g; Fiber 1.6g; Sugar 8.55g; Protein 55.33g

# Spiced Beef Stew with Parsley

## Prep Time: 10 minutes | Cook time: 35 minutes | Servings: 4

### Ingredients:

1 red onion, chopped

1 tablespoon balsamic vinegar

2 tablespoons coconut oil, melted

A pinch of sea salt and black pepper

1 pound beef, ground

3 garlic cloves, minced

⅔ teaspoon ginger, grated

1 teaspoon coriander seeds

1 teaspoon cumin, ground

1 teaspoon sweet paprika

3 cups sweet potatoes, peeled and cubed

1 and ½ cups veggie stock

1 carrot, chopped

10 oz fresh tomatoes, peeled, chopped

¼ cup parsley, chopped

Zest of 1 lemon, grated

### Instructions:

1. Heat up a large saucepan with the oil over medium heat, add the onion, stir and sauté for 10 minutes. 2. Add vinegar, stir and cook for 1 minute more. 3. Add ginger and the meat, stir and cook for 2 minutes. 4. Add garlic, coriander, cumin, and paprika, stir and cook for 2 minutes. 5. Add stock, carrot, tomatoes and lemon zest, stir, cover and cook for 20 minutes. 6. Add parsley, stir, cook for 2 minutes more, divide into bowls and serve. 7. Enjoy!

Per Serving: Calories 270; Fat 13.97g; Sodium 146mg; Carbs 13g; Fiber 3.8g; Sugar 3.49g; Protein 25.97g

# Pork Chops in Tomato Sauce

## Prep Time: 15 minutes | Cook Time: 40 minutes | Servings: 4

### Ingredients:

4 pork chops

1 onion, chopped

1 bell pepper, chopped

1 (15 ounce) can tomato sauce

garlic powder to taste

salt and pepper to taste

### Instructions:

1. Pour enough oil to cover the bottom of a big skillet and heat on moderately high heat. Dip into flour with pork chops, then put into pan and brown both sides well. Take chops out and put aside. 2. Put in bell pepper and onion, then cook while stirring until nearly softened, about 5 minutes. Turn the pork chops back to skillet and put in the tomato sauce. Let the sauce begin bubbling, then lower heat to low. 3. Simmer for a half hour and use pepper, salt and garlic powder to season to taste.

Per Serving: Calories 368; Fat 17.72g; Sodium 219mg; Carbs 8.96g; Fiber 3g; Sugar 5.19g; Protein 41.93g

# Cajun Garlicky Pulled Pork

## Prep Time: 15 minutes | Cook Time: 6-8 hours | Servings: 8

**Ingredients:**

2 teaspoons Cajun seasoning
1 (3 pound) pork shoulder roast
½ (16 ounce) jar golden pepperoncini, undrained
2 teaspoons adobo sauce

1 yellow onion, chopped
3 cloves garlic
½ cup fresh cilantro leaves
water as needed

**Instructions:**

1. Rub into the pork shoulder with Cajun seasoning, put in the bottom of a slow cooker. 2. Pour over the pork with adobo sauce and pepperoncini with the juice. Put cilantro, garlic and onion on top. Add enough water into the slow cooker until the water covers the bottom of the pork shoulder by ½. 3. Cook for about 6-8 hours on Low until the meat starts to fall apart. Right inside the slow cooker; use 2 forks to shred the meat before eating.

**Per Serving:** Calories 228; Fat 10.55g; Sodium 112mg; Carbs 3.2g; Fiber 0.6g; Sugar 1.69g; Protein 28.32g

# Pork and Rutabaga Stew

## Prep Time: 15 minutes | Cook Time: 8 hours | Servings: 8

**Ingredients:**

2½ pounds boneless pork chops
1 (14-ouncecan diced tomatoes
4 cups chicken broth
2 garlic cloves
1½ teaspoons dried oregano
½ teaspoon cumin
2 tablespoons butter

1½ cups rutabaga, peeled and cubed
½ cup onions, chopped
1 tablespoon chili powder
1 teaspoon kosher salt
½ teaspoon black pepper
3 tablespoons lemon juice

**Instructions:**

1. Mix together all of the ingredients in a large slow cooker and stir well. 2. Cook on LOW for about 8 hours and dish out the pork. 3. Shred with fork and return to the pot. 4. Squeeze lime and serve hot.

**Per Serving:** Calories 418; Fat 16.35g; Sodium 916mg; Carbs 6.1g; Fiber 1.4g; Sugar 1.71g; Protein 58.61g

# Yummy Lamb Stew

Prep Time: 10 minutes | Cook time: 2 hours | Servings: 4

**Ingredients:**

1 and ½ pounds lamb meat, cubed

1 tablespoon olive oil

1 small red chili pepper, chopped

1 yellow onion, chopped

3 garlic cloves, minced

2 celery sticks, chopped

2 and ½ teaspoons garam masala

1 and ¼ teaspoons turmeric powder

1 and ½ cups coconut milk

1 and ½ teaspoons ghee

1 and ½ tablespoons tomato paste

2 carrots, chopped

1 cup water

A pinch of sea salt and black pepper

1 tablespoon lemon juice

1 tablespoon cilantro, chopped

**Instructions:**

1. Heat up a large saucepan with the oil over medium-high heat, add the lamb, and brown for 4 minutes on all sides. 2. Add celery, chili and onion, stir and cook for 1 minute. 3. Reduce the heat to medium, add turmeric, garam masala, garlic and the ghee, stir and cook for 2 minutes more. 4. Add tomato paste, coconut milk, water, salt and pepper, stir, bring to a boil, cover and cook for 1 hour. 5. Add carrots, stir, cover saucepan again and cook for 40 minutes more. 6. Add lemon juice and parsley, stir, divide into bowls and serve hot. 7. Enjoy!

**Per Serving:** Calories 374; Fat 26.74g; Sodium 180mg; Carbs 14.1g; Fiber 4.1g; Sugar 6.86g; Protein 21.75g

# BBQ Rack Ribs On the Grill

Prep Time: 15 minutes | Cook Time: 2 hours | Servings: 8

**Ingredients:**

2 racks ribs, membrane on bone side removed

1 tablespoon steak seasoning, or to taste

1 cup water, or more as needed

½ cup barbeque sauce, or to taste

**Instructions:**

1. Preheat the grill for low heat. 2. Halve the ribs and add steak seasoning to season. Put the ribs in a foil pan, bone-side facing down; pour in water. Cover the pan using an aluminum foil sheet. 3. On the prepped grill, let the ribs cook for 1½ to 2 ½ hours, putting water after every hour in case liquid has vaporized. To ribs, put the barbeque sauce and continue to cook for an additional of 30 minutes. An instant-read thermometer pricked into the middle should register 145°F.

**Per Serving:** Calories 846; Fat 72.98g; Sodium 325mg; Carbs 1.72g; Fiber 0.4g; Sugar 0.76g; Protein 42.15g

# Apple & Cranberry Stuffed Pork Chops

Prep Time: 15 minutes | Cook Time: 1 hour 16 minutes | Servings: 2

**Ingredients:**

1 tablespoon olive oil

½ onion, chopped

1 large Granny Smith apple - peeled, cored and diced

2 tablespoons balsamic vinegar

½ cup dried cranberries

salt and pepper to taste

2 (6 ounce) boneless pork chops

1 tablespoon olive oil

**Instructions:**

1. In a skillet over medium heat, heat 1 tablespoon olive oil. Mix in apple and onion; cook while stirring for 5 minutes. Mix in balsamic vinegar and cranberries and keep cooking until the onions and apple are tender, about 5 more minutes. 2. Sprinkle with pepper and salt to season; on a plate, scrape the mixture and refrigerate to cold. 3. Set oven to 350°F to preheat. 4. In a small baking dish, lightly grease. Use a thin bladed knife to cut a large pocket into the pork chops. 5. In the pork chops, stuff the cooled apple mixture and use toothpicks to secure (if needed). In a large skillet, heat leftover 1 tablespoon of olive oil over medium-high heat. 6. Sprinkle the pork chops with pepper and salt to taste, and put into the hot skillet. Cook for 3 minutes per side until brown, then place into a baking dish. 7. Add the leftover apple mixture on top and use aluminum foil to cover the baking dish. 8. Bake in prepared oven for about 40 minutes depending on the thick of pork chops, until the center of the pork remains no pink. 9. Bake without a cover for 10 more minutes until the edges of apple mixture have browned.

Per Serving: Calories 482; Fat 20.16g; Sodium 100mg; Carbs 29.99g; Fiber 3.7g; Sugar 22.09g; Protein 42.74g

# Tangy Minute Steaks

Prep Time: 15 minutes | Cook Time: 1 hour | Servings: 1

**Ingredients:**

4 (½ pound) cube steaks (pounded round meat)

1 (10.5 ounce) can condensed French onion soup

**Instructions:**

1. Set the oven to 350°F to preheat. 2. Brown the cube steaks briefly in a big skillet on moderate heat. 3. In a 13"x9" baking dish, arrange one single layer of meat and drizzle over top with soup. In the preheated oven, bake about an hour.

Per Serving: Calories 435; Fat 22.2g; Sodium 1405mg; Carbs 6.4g; Fiber 1.3g; Sugar 0g; Protein 49.9g

# Greek Pulled Pork with Pepperoncini Peppers

Prep Time: 10 minutes | Cook Time: 4 hours 15 minutes | Servings: 6

**Ingredients:**

1 (2 pound) pork tenderloin, fat trimmed

2 tablespoons Greek seasoning (such as Cavender's®), or more to taste

1 (16 ounce) jar sliced pepperoncini peppers (such as Mezzetta®)

**Instructions:**

1. Put pork tenderloin into a slow cooker, generously dust meat with Greek seasoning, and then pour the peperoncini peppers jar with their juice over the pork. 2. Cook on High for 4 hours. 3. Shred the pork with 2 forks, let cook for another 10 to 15 more minutes.

Per Serving: Calories 260; Fat 5.39g; Sodium 292mg; Carbs 10.77g; Fiber 0.8g; Sugar 8.1g; Protein 40.06g

# Herbed Beef Roast

Prep Time: 15 minutes | Cook Time: 35 minutes | Servings: 4

**Ingredients:**

2 tablespoons fresh rosemary

2 tablespoons fresh thyme leaves

2 bay leaves

4 cloves garlic

1 large shallot, peeled and quartered

1 tablespoon grated orange zest

1 tablespoon coarse salt

1 teaspoon freshly ground black pepper

½ teaspoon ground nutmeg

¼ teaspoon ground cloves

2 tablespoons olive oil

2 (2 pound) beef tenderloin roasts, trimmed

**Instructions:**

1. Put cloves, nutmeg, pepper, salt, orange zest, shallot, garlic, bay leaves, thyme and rosemary in a food processor. While adding oil, run machine; process till smooth. Evenly spread mixture on all tenderloin's sides; put beef into big glass baking dish. Use foil to cover; refrigerate for a minimum of 6 hours. 2. Preheat an oven to 400°F; put tenderloins onto rack in a big roasting pan. 3. In preheated oven, roast beef for 35 minutes till inserted meat thermometer in middle of beef reads 140°F. Remove from the oven; loosely cover with foil and allow to stand about 10 minutes. Cut beef; serve.

Per Serving: Calories 514; Fat 26.63g; Sodium 1881mg; Carbs 2.65g; Fiber 0.6g; Sugar 0.56g; Protein 66.25g

# Beef and Potato Hash

## Prep Time: 10 minutes | Cook Time: 30 minutes | Servings: 6

**Ingredients:**

6 large potatoes, peeled and diced

1 (12 ounce) can corned beef, cut into chunks

1 medium onion, chopped

1 cup beef broth

**Instructions:**

1. Simmer beef broth, onion, corned beef and potatoes, covered, in big deep skillet on medium heat till liquid is nearly gone and potatoes are at mashing consistency; stir well then serve.

Per Serving: Calories 378; Fat 4.06g; Sodium 79mg; Carbs 66.18g; Fiber 8.4g; Sugar 3.66g; Protein 21g

# Citrus Beef and Fruit Kabobs

## Prep Time: 25 minutes | Cook Time: 10 minutes | Servings: 4

**Ingredients:**

1-pound beef top sirloin steak boneless, cut 1-inch thick

¼ cup chopped fresh cilantro leaves

1 tablespoon smoked paprika

1 medium orange

¼ teaspoon ground red pepper (optional)

4 cups cubed mango, watermelon, peaches and/or plums

Salt

**Instructions:**

1. Grate orange peel; squeeze the juice from the orange and measure 2 tablespoons, set aside. In a small mixing bowl, combine ground red pepper, paprika, cilantro, and orange peel. Slice beef steak into pieces, about 1 ¼ inches. 2. Combine beef with 2 ½ tablespoons cilantro mixture together in a food-safe plastic bag; turn until evenly coated. Put fruit and the remaining cilantro mixture into another food-safe plastic bag; turn until evenly coated. 3. Seal the bags tightly. Let fruit and beef marinate for 15 to 120 minutes in the fridge. 4. Steep eight 9-inch bamboo skewers in water for 10 minutes; drain. Thread beef evenly onto 4 bamboo skewers, slightly spacing between beef pieces. Skewer fruit onto the remaining 4 individual skewers. 5. Transfer kabobs on grid over medium, ash-covered coals. Cover and grill beef kabobs for 8 to 10 minutes (or 9 to 11 minutes over medium heat on preheated gas grill) for medium rare (145°F) to medium (160°F), turning once in a while. Grill fruit kabobs, turning once, until tender and starting to brown for 5 to 7 minutes. 6. Sprinkle salt as desired over beef to season. Spoon the reserved 2 tablespoons orange juice over fruit kabobs before serving.

Per Serving: Calories 259; Fat 7.36g; Sodium 683mg; Carbs 26.55g; Fiber 3.3g; Sugar 23.36g; Protein 24.79g

# Beef Pot Roast and Potato Stew

**Prep Time: 15 minutes | Cook Time: 4 hours | Servings: 8**

**Ingredients:**

1 tablespoon salt

1 tablespoon ground black pepper

2 teaspoons dried parsley

2 teaspoons dried oregano

2 pounds beef pot roast

4 potatoes, cut into chunks

2 cups baby carrots

1 tomato, cut into chunks

½ yellow onion, cut into chunks

1 (6.5 ounce) can tomato sauce

½ cup water

**Instructions:**

1. Season beef pot roast evenly with salt, parsley, black pepper, and oregano. 2. Transfer roast in a slow cooker with the tomato, carrots, potatoes, and onion on top of the beef. Pour water and tomato sauce on top of the veggies and beef. 3. Over high heat, cook for 4 hours.

**Per Serving:** Calories 349; Fat 9.58g; Sodium 1029mg; Carbs 38.68g; Fiber 6g; Sugar 4.13g; Protein 28.65g

# Simple Roast Beef

**Prep Time: 5 minutes | Cook Time: 1 hour | Servings: 6**

**Ingredients:**

3 pounds beef eye of round roast

½ teaspoon kosher salt

½ teaspoon garlic powder

¼ teaspoon freshly ground black pepper

**Instructions:**

1. Start preheating the oven to 375°F. For the untied roast, use a cotton twine to tie at 3-in. intervals. In a pan, put the roast, use pepper, garlic powder, and salt to season. Adjust the season to taste. 2. Roast for 60 minutes in the oven (20 minutes each pound). Take out of the oven, use foil to loosely cover, and then let stand for 15-20 minutes.

**Per Serving:** Calories 380; Fat 10.15g; Sodium 346mg; Carbs 0.19g; Fiber 0g; Sugar 0g; Protein 67.36g

# Baby Back Ribs with Apple & BBQ Sauce

## Prep Time: 15 minutes | Cook Time: 1 hour 30minutes | Servings: 8

**Ingredients:**

4 cups barbeque sauce

4 cups applesauce

4 pounds baby back pork ribs

salt and black pepper to taste

cayenne pepper to taste

garlic powder to taste

**Instructions:**

1. In a bowl, mix the applesauce and barbeque sauce. Lay the ribs on the heavy-duty aluminum large foil sheet. 2. Rub the garlic powder, cayenne pepper, pepper, and salt all over the sides of the ribs. 3. Drizzle over the sauce until the ribs are well coated. Seal the ribs in the foil. Marinate for 8 hours or overnight inside the fridge. 4. Set the grill to high heat for preheating. 5. Arrange the foil with ribs on the grill grate. Cook for 1 hour. 6. Remove the ribs from the foil and lay them directly on the grill grate. Cook for 30 more minutes, basting often with the sauce until the ribs are done.

Per Serving: Calories 412; Fat 13.16g; Sodium 1072mg; Carbs 23.73g; Fiber 3.9g; Sugar 17.16g; Protein 49.56g

# Spicy Barbequed Steak

## Prep Time: 15 minutes | Cook Time: 10 minutes | Servings: 8

**Ingredients:**

¼ cup chili sauce

¼ cup fish sauce

1½ tablespoons dark sesame oil

1 tablespoon grated fresh ginger root

3 cloves garlic, peeled and crushed

2 pounds flank steak

**Instructions:**

1. Whisk garlic, ginger, sesame oil, fish sauce and chili sauce together in a medium bowl. Reserve several tablespoons of the mixture for brushing steaks when grilling. Then score the flank steak and transfer into a shallow dish. Add the remaining marinade on top of the steak and then flip to coat. Cover the dish and place in fridge to marinate for at least three hours. 2. Preheat the outdoor grill over high heat. 3. Brush the grilling surface lightly with oil. Then grill the steak for about five minutes on each side or to the doneness desired. Be sure to brush often with reserved marinade mixture.

Per Serving: Calories 192; Fat 8.26g; Sodium 881mg; Carbs 2.52g; Fiber 0.5g; Sugar 1.25g; Protein 25.06g

# Spicy Beef and Greens Stew

Prep Time: 10 minutes | Cook time: 8 hours | Servings: 4

**Ingredients:**

2 and ½ pounds beef chuck, cubed

3 cups collard greens

3 cups water

3 tablespoons allspice

¼ cup garlic powder

⅓ cup sweet paprika

1 teaspoon cayenne pepper

1 teaspoon chili powder

**Instructions:**

1. In a slow cooker, combine all of the ingredients, toss, cover and cook on Low for 8 hours. 2. Divide into bowls and serve. 3. Enjoy!

**Per Serving:** Calories 383; Fat 14.91g; Sodium 238mg; Carbs 17.2g; Fiber 6.4g; Sugar 1.38g; Protein 50.65g

# Lemony Barbecue Pork Chops

Prep Time: 10 minutes | Cook Time: 25 minutes | Servings: 4

**Ingredients:**

2 cups barbecue sauce

4 pork chops

1 lemon, juiced

**Instructions:**

1. Pour enough barbecue sauce to coat chops in a bowl or shallow dish. Put chops and smother into sauce to coat evenly. 2. Put coated chops over medium-high heat in a medium skillet and sauté until thoroughly cooked, 20 to 25 minutes, scattering lemon juice generously over both sides of chops while cooking. 3. Put off the heat and serve.

**Per Serving:** Calories 577; Fat 18.29g; Sodium 1555mg; Carbs 59.13g; Fiber 1.3g; Sugar 47.84g; Protein 41.42g

# Beef and Carrot Stock

Prep Time: 25 minutes | Cook Time: 5 hours 45 minutes | Servings: 8

**Ingredients:**

6 pounds beef soup bones

1 large onion

3 large carrots

½ cup water

2 stalks celery, including some leaves

1 large tomato

½ cup chopped parsnip

1 medium potato

8 whole black peppercorns

4 sprigs fresh parsley

1 bay leaf

1 tablespoon salt

2 teaspoons dried thyme

2 cloves garlic

12 cups water

**Instructions:**

1. Preheat the oven to 450ºF. 2. Cut the root end of the onion. Quarter or slice onion, and peel all. Clean the carrots, cut into 1-inch chunks. Place soup bones, onion, and carrots in a large shallow roasting pan. Bake until the bones are well browned, uncovered, about 30 minutes, seldom turning. 3. Allow to drain off the fat. In a large soup pot or Dutch oven, put the carrots, onion, and browned bones. Add ½ cup water to the roasting pan and rinse. Then pour this liquid back into the soup pot. 4. Next, clean the potato and cut into chunks, peel them all. Slice the celery stalks into 3 parts. Place garlic, thyme, salt, bay leaf, parsley (including stems), peppercorns, potato, parsnip, tomato, and celery into the pot. Then pour in 12 cups of water. 5. Next, bring the mixture to a boil. Reduce the flame. Put a lid on and simmer for 5 hours. Filter the stock. Remove the seasonings, vegetables, and meat. 6. To refine the stock for a clear soup: Combine 1 crushed eggshell, 1 egg white, and ¼ cup cold water in order to eliminate the solid flecks which are too small to be filtered out with a cheesecloth. Add to the filtered stock. Next, bring to a boil. Then take away from the heat, let sit for 5 minutes. Through a sieve lined with cheesecloth, strain again.

**Per Serving:** Calories 789; Fat 35.54g; Sodium 1136mg; Carbs 15.45g; Fiber 3g; Sugar 3.55g; Protein 96.62g

# Chapter 5 Fish and Seafood Recipes

# Tangy Sea Bass and Potato Stew

### Prep Time: 10 minutes | Cook Time: 15 minutes | Servings: 4

**Ingredients:**

1 red onion, diced

4 tbsp olive oil

½ cup chicken broth

1 cup clam juice

½ pound potatoes, peeled and cubed

2 ½ cups water

14 ounces canned diced tomatoes

1½ pounds sea bass fillets, chopped

1 tsp minced garlic

2 tbsp chopped dill

2 tbsp lemon juice

Salt and pepper, to taste

**Instructions:**

1. Turn the Instant Pot on and set it to "SAUTE". 2. Add half of the oil and heat it until sizzling. When hot enough, add the onions and cook for 3 minutes. Add the garlic and saute for a minute. Pour the broth over and deglaze the bottom of the pot. Stir in the tomatoes, potatoes, water, and clam juice. 3. Close the lid and turn clockwise to seal. Select the "MANUAL" cooking mode. Set the cooking time to 5 minutes. Cook on HIGH pressure. 4. When the timer goes off, hit "KEEP WARM/ CANCEL" to turn the Instant Pot off. Move the pressure handle to "Venting" to do a quick pressure release. Open the lid carefully and add the sea bass pieces. 5. Close and seal the lid again and cook on "MANUAL" for another 5 minutes. Again, turn the Instant Pot off, do a quick pressure release, and open the lid. Press the "SAUTE" button. 6. Stir in the remaining ingredients (along with the rest of the oil), and cook for 3 more minutes with the lid off. Ladle into serving bowls immediately. 7. Enjoy!

**Per Serving:** Calories 449; Fat 19.96g; Sodium 624mg; Carbs 26.45g; Fiber 4.8g; Sugar 7.14g; Protein 41.19g

# Delicious Tilapia in Stewed Tomatoes

### Prep Time: 10 minutes | Cook Time: 20 minutes | Servings:4

**Ingredients:**

1 (14.5 ounce) can stewed tomatoes

4 (4 ounce) tilapia fillets

**Instructions:**

1. Heat tomatoes in big skillet on medium heat till simmering; add tilapia. 2. Put tomatoes on tilapia to coat and cover skillet. Simmer for 10 minutes till fish easily flakes with a fork.

**Per Serving:** Calories 129; Fat 2.24g; Sodium 185mg; Carbs 3.77g; Fiber 2.1g; Sugar 2.77g; Protein 24.15g

# Tiger Prawns with Cocktail Sauce

## Prep Time: 15 minutes | Cook Time: 25 minutes | Servings: 3

**Ingredients:**

1 quart water

1 pound tiger prawns with shell

3 ounces Old Bay Seasoning

1 (12 ounce) jar cocktail sauce

**Instructions:**

1. Boil a quart of water in a big pot. 2. In a steamer basket, put in shrimp. Place the steamer over the pot then cover; avoid immersing the shrimp. If needed, get rid of some of the water. Sprinkle Old Bay seasoning to season. 3. Cook shrimp in the steamer until pink. 4. Consume shrimps by discarding the shells as you go. Use cocktail sauce as a dip.

**Per Serving:** Calories 407; Fat 8.82g; Sodium 2845mg; Carbs 56.67g; Fiber 9.6g; Sugar 15.74g; Protein 33.09g

# Black Olives & Carrot Crab Cakes

## Prep Time: 10 minutes | Cook Time: 4 minutes | Servings: 2

**Ingredients:**

1 cup crab meat

¼ cup chopped black olives

1 carrot, shredded

½ cup boiled and mashed potatoes

¼ cup almond flour

¼ cup grated onion

1½ cups canned diced tomatoes

1 tbsp olive oil

¼ cup chicken broth

**Instructions:**

1. Place the crab meat, carrots, olives, flour, potatoes, and onion, in a bowl. Mix with your hands until the mixture is fully incorporated. 2. Shape the mixture into two patties. 3. Add the olive oil to the Instant Pot and set it to "SAUTE". 4. When hot and sizzling, add the crab cakes and cook for a minute. 5. Flip them over and cook for another minute. 6. Pour the tomatoes and broth over and close the lid. Turn it clockwise to seal properly. 7. Select the "MANUAL" cooking mode and set the cooking time to 2 minutes. Cook on HIGH pressure. 8. When the timer goes off, select "KEEP WARM/CANCEL". 9. Turn the pressure handle to "Venting" for a quick pressure release and open the lid carefully. 10. Serve and enjoy!

**Per Serving:** Calories 335; Fat 12.17g; Sodium 282mg; Carbs 34.57g; Fiber 11.4g; Sugar 5.33g; Protein 25.53g

# Gingered Lime Salmon

Prep Time: 15 minutes | Cook Time: 20 minutes | Servings: 4

**Ingredients:**

1 (1½-pound) salmon fillet

1 tablespoon olive oil

1 teaspoon seafood seasoning (such as Old Bay®)

1 teaspoon ground black pepper

1 (1 inch) piece fresh ginger root, peeled and thinly sliced

6 cloves garlic, minced

1 lime, thinly sliced

**Instructions:**

1. Position oven rack approximately 6 to 8 inches away from the heat source and preheat broiler; set oven's broiler to Low setting if there is. Line aluminum foil over a baking sheet. 2. Arrange salmon on the prepared baking sheet, skin side down; rub olive oil over the salmon. Season fish with black pepper and seafood seasoning. Place ginger slices on top of salmon and scatter garlic over. Arrange lime slices over ginger-garlic layer. 3. Broil salmon for about 10 minutes until heated through and starting to turn opaque; watch carefully. Turn broiler to high setting if there is; keep broiling for 5 to 10 minutes longer or until salmon is thoroughly cooked and easily flaked using a fork.

Per Serving: Calories 304; Fat 15.63g; Sodium 790mg; Carbs 3.4g; Fiber 0.4g; Sugar 0.32g; Protein 35.54g

# Poached Whitefish in Tomato Saffron Broth

Prep Time: 10 minutes | Cook Time: 25 minutes | Servings: 6

**Ingredients:**

1 tablespoon olive oil

2 bulbs fennel, chopped

1 onion, chopped

1½ pounds whitefish fillets

1 pinch saffron

1 tablespoon fennel seeds

1 cup diced tomatoes

1 cup water, or more as needed

**Instructions:**

1. Put a skillet on medium heat and heat olive oil. Add onion and fennel bulbs into the skillet; stir and cook in about 5 minutes until the onion turns translucent and softened. 2. Add water, tomatoes, fennel seeds, saffron and whitefish. Boil while covering; then take it out of the heat. 3. Set it aside to sit with cover for about 10 minutes until the fish can be flaked out easily with a fork.

Per Serving: Calories 389; Fat 23.05g; Sodium 600mg; Carbs 19.31g; Fiber 10.3g; Sugar 5.4g; Protein 27.66g

# Creamy Tilapia

## Prep Time: 10 minutes | Cook Time: 3 hours | Servings: 3

**Ingredients:**

¾ cup homemade chicken broth

1 pound tilapia fillets

1 cup sour cream

Salt and black pepper, to taste

1 teaspoon cayenne pepper

**Instructions:**

1. Put tilapia fillets in the slow cooker along with rest of the ingredients. 2. Cover the lid and cook on low for about 3 hours. 3. Dish out and serve hot.

Per Serving: Calories 261; Fat 10.98g; Sodium 431mg; Carbs 7.54g; Fiber 0.5g; Sugar 1.57g; Protein 33.74g

# Thai-Style Pumpkin Seafood Stew

## Prep Time: 15 minutes | Cook Time: 35 minutes | Servings: 12

**Ingredients:**

1½ tablespoons fresh galangal, roughly chopped

1 teaspoon lime zest

1 small kabocha squash

32 medium-sized mussels, fresh and alive

1 pound shrimp

16 leaves Thai basil

1 (13.5-ouncecancoconut milk

1 tablespoon lemongrass, minced

4 garlic cloves, roughly chopped

32 medium-sizedclams, fresh and alive

1½ pounds fresh salmon

2 tablespoons coconut oil

Salt and black pepper, to taste

**Instructions:**

1. Add coconut milk, lemongrass, galangal, garlic and lime leaves in a small saucepan, and bring to a boil. 2. Allow to simmer for about 25 minutes, stirring occasionally. 3. Strain this mixture through a fine sieve into a soup pot and bring to a simmer. 4. Meanwhile, heat oil in a pan and add kabocha squash. 5. Season with a bit of salt and black pepper and sauté for about 5 minutes. 6. Add this mixture to the coconut milk mixture. 7. Heat oil again in a pan and add fish and shrimp. 8. Season with salt and pepper and sauté for about 4 minutes. 9. Throw this mixture into the coconut milk mixture along with clams and mussels. 10. Simmer for about 8 minutes and garnish with Thai basil to serve.

Per Serving: Calories 231; Fat 9.79g; Sodium 493mg; Carbs 4.54g; Fiber 0.6g; Sugar 1.53g; Protein 29.97g

# Cod in Ginger Tamarind Sauce

## Prep Time: 10 minutes | Cook Time: 30 minutes | Servings: 4

**Ingredients:**

1 tablespoon cooking oil

1 teaspoon mustard seed

2 tablespoons chopped fresh ginger

1 cup chopped onions

2 cups water

1 tablespoon tamarind paste

2 tablespoons coriander powder

½ teaspoon ground red pepper

Salt to taste

½ pound cod fillets, cut into 1 inch cubes

Fresh curry leaves (optional)

**Instructions:**

1. In a saucepan, heat oil on medium-high heat. In hot oil, cook mustard seeds until they start to crackle. Mix in onion and ginger. Cook for 5 minutes. 2. Put water and mix in tamarind paste. Boil. Season with salt, chile powder, and coriander. Lower heat to medium-low. Cook for 15 minutes, occasionally mixing. 3. In sauce, cook fish until fish has cooked through. Top with fresh curry leaves. Serve.

**Per Serving:** Calories 215; Fat 14.97g; Sodium 864mg; Carbs 9.86g; Fiber 4.4g; Sugar 2.29g; Protein 13.63g

# Tropical Shrimp Stew

## Prep Time: 10 minutes | Cook Time: 13 minutes | Servings: 6

**Ingredients:**

1 garlic clove, minced

¼ cup onions, diced

¼ cup olive oil

1½ pounds raw shrimp, peeled & deveined

¼ cup red pepper, roasted and diced

1 (14 ozcan diced tomatoes with chilies

2 tablespoons lemon juice

2 tablespoons Sriracha hot sauce

1 cup coconut milk

¼ cup fresh cilantro, chopped

Salt and black pepper, to taste

**Instructions:**

1. Heat the oil in a medium saucepan and add garlic and onions. 2. Sauté for about 3 minutes and add peppers, tomatoes, shrimp and cilantro. 3. Simmer for about 5 minutes and add coconut milk and Sriracha sauce. 4. Cook for about 5 minutes and stir in lime juice, salt and black pepper. 5. Garnish with fresh cilantro and serve hot.

**Per Serving:** Calories 237; Fat 12g; Sodium 1426mg; Carbs 6.53g; Fiber 0.4g; Sugar 3.24g; Protein 25.2g

# Coconut Prawns and Okra

## Prep Time: 15 minutes | Cook Time: 25 minutes | Servings:3

**Ingredients:**

½ pound prawns, peeled and deveined

Sea salt to taste

½ cup grated coconut

4 Kashmiri chile peppers

1 tablespoon coriander seeds

3 cloves garlic, peeled

5 peppercorns

1 tablespoon vegetable oil

1 small onion, sliced

3 ounces okra (bindhi), cut into thirds

¼ teaspoon ground turmeric

3 pieces kokum (fruit from the mangosteen family)

1½ cups water, or as needed

**Instructions:**

1. Season prawns with sea salt. 2. Using a mortar and pestle to crush peppercorns, garlic, coriander seeds, chile peppers, and coconut together until the masala is evenly orange. 3. In a pot, heat oil over medium heat, stir and cook the onion for 5-10 minutes until slightly browned and tender. Stir turmeric and masala into the onion, cook for 1 minute until aromatic. Fill with enough water to create a creamy and substantial gravy. 4. Boil the gravy, add okra and prawns and cook for 10 minutes until the okra is soft and the prawns are heated through. Mix kokum in the prawn mixture and boil again. Take the pot away from the heat and let sit.

**Per Serving:** Calories 110; Fat 6.24g; Sodium 845mg; Carbs 13.82g; Fiber 3.4g; Sugar 4.07g; Protein 2.16g

# Lemony Coconut Cod Curry

## Prep Time: 35 minutes | Cook Time: 25 minutes | Servings: 6

**Ingredients:**

1 onion, chopped

2 pounds cod

1 cup dry coconut, chopped

Salt and black pepper, to taste

1 cup fresh lemon juice

**Instructions:**

1. Put the cod along with all other ingredients in a pressure cooker. 2. Add 2 cups of water and cover the lid. 3. Cook on High Pressure for about 25 minutes and naturally release the pressure. 4. Open the lid and dish out the curry to serve hot.

**Per Serving:** Calories 201; Fat 6.26g; Sodium 529mg; Carbs 12.65g; Fiber 0.3g; Sugar 9.03g; Protein 23.99g

# Baked Tilapia with Tapenade

## Prep Time: 10 minutes | Cook Time: 15 minutes | Servings:2

### Ingredients:

4 (6 ounce) tilapia fillets
1 tablespoon olive oil
½ cup chopped tomatoes
5 pitted Kalamata olives, chopped

1 tablespoon chopped onion
1 tablespoon capers
Salt and ground black pepper to taste

### Instructions:

1. Preheat oven at 375°F. Set tilapia fillets on a baking sheet and apply olive oil. 2. Bake tilapia for 10 - 15 minutes in the preheated oven, till it looks opaque and can be flaked with pork. 3. In a tiny saucepan, combine capers, onion, olives, and chopped tomatoes. Cook at medium-high heat for 5-10 minutes, stir infrequently, till the tomatoes split and tapenade flavors mingle. Garnish baked fillets with tapenade.

Per Serving: Calories 311; Fat 11.89g; Sodium 330mg; Carbs 4.51g; Fiber 1.2g; Sugar 2.39g; Protein 47.59g

# Lemony Halibut

## Prep Time: 15 minutes | Cook Time: 30 minutes | Servings: 6

### Ingredients:

6 (6 ounce) halibut fillets
1 tablespoon dried dill weed
1 tablespoon onion powder
2 teaspoons dried parsley
¼ teaspoon paprika

2 tablespoons lemon juice
1 pinch seasoned salt, or more to taste
1 pinch garlic powder
1 pinch lemon pepper

### Instructions:

1. Prepare oven for preheating at 375°F. 2. Prepare foil and cut into 6 squares. It must be large enough for each fillet. 3. Place fillet at the middle of the foil square. Drizzle onion powder, paprika, dill weed, lemon pepper, garlic powder, seasoned salt and parsley on each fillet. Squeeze lemon juice on each fillet and wrap over with foil to create a pocket. Seal edges by folding foil. Prepare baking sheets and transfer sealed packets. 4. Place in preheated oven. For 30 minutes, cook until fish flakes easily with a fork.

Per Serving: Calories 255; Fat 15.37g; Sodium 812mg; Carbs 9.66g; Fiber 5.5g; Sugar 0.91g; Protein 20.01g

# Tasty Baked Tilapia

**Prep Time: 30 minutes | Cook Time: 30 minutes | Servings: 2**

**Ingredients:**

2 (4 ounce) fillets tilapia

¼ cup sesame oil

1 clove garlic, minced

1 teaspoon Italian seasoning

Kosher salt to taste

Fresh ground black pepper to taste

**Instructions:**

1. In a bowl, add the tilapia and drizzle the sesame oil over. Use pepper, kosher salt, Italian seasoning and garlic for seasoning. Cover and put in the fridge for at least half an hour to let it marinate. 2. Set an oven at 350°F and start preheating. 3. Move the marinade and tilapia to a baking tray, put in the oven and start baking for 30 minutes, until the fish can be easily shredded with a fork.

**Per Serving:** Calories 368; Fat 29.27g; Sodium 1329mg; Carbs 3.47g; Fiber 0.6g; Sugar 1.32g; Protein 23.9g

# Tilapia Potato Chowder

**Prep Time: 10 minutes | Cook Time: 15 minutes | Servings: 4**

**Ingredients:**

1⅓ cups water

1 cup almond milk

1 cup peeled and chopped potatoes

⅔ pounds tilapia, chopped

½ cups chopped celery

⅔ cup chicken stock

¾ cup diced onion

¼ tsp salt

¼ tsp pepper

¼ tsp onion powder

1 tbsp arrowroot mixed with 1½ tbsp water

**Instructions:**

1. Combine everything except for the arrowroot mixture in your Instant Pot. 2. Close the lid and turn clockwise to seal. 3. Select "MANUAL" and set the cooking time to 10 minutes. Cook on HIGH pressure. 4. When the timer goes off, press the "KEEP WARM/CANCEL" button. 5. Do a quick pressure release by turning the pressure handle to "Venting". Ensuring to keep your hands away from the steam. 6. Set the Instant Pot to "SAUTE". 7. Stir in the arrowroot mixture and cook for about 5 minutes, or until the chowder is thickened. 8. Serve immediately and enjoy!

**Per Serving:** Calories 162; Fat 3.07g; Sodium 289mg; Carbs 14.27g; Fiber 1.5g; Sugar 5.82g; Protein 19.49g

# Lime-Garlic Shrimp Salad

Prep Time: 15 minutes | Cook Time: 20 minutes | Servings: 4

## Ingredients:

1 lime
3 cloves garlic, minced
1 pound large fresh shrimp, peeled and deveined
¾ cup Swanson® Chicken Broth or Swanson® Chicken Stock
1 medium orange bell pepper or red bell

pepper, cut into 2-inch long strips
1 small onion, cut in half and sliced
¼ cup chopped fresh cilantro leaves
4 cups romaine lettuce or iceberg lettuce, torn into bite-sized pieces
2 large tomatoes, thickly sliced
¼ teaspoon ground black pepper

## Instructions:

1. Grate 2 teaspoons of lime zest and squeeze 1 tablespoon of lime juice. 2. In a gallon-size resealable plastic bag or a 2-quart shallow, nonmetallic baking dish, stir together garlic, lime zest and lime juice. Add the shrimp to the mixture and toss until well coated. Seal the bag or cover the dish and refrigerate for 30 minutes, remember to flip several times while marinating. 3. In a 2-quart saucepan, heat the broth over medium-high heat to a boil. Add onion and pepper and cook until vegetables become tender-crisp, remember to stir occasionally. 4. Lower the heat to medium. Add shrimp and marinade into the saucepan and heat to a boil. Cook until the shrimps are well cooked. Stir in cilantro. 5. Divide shrimp mixture, tomatoes and lettuce among 4 serving plates. Sprinkle with black pepper to season.
Per Serving: Calories 181; Fat 4.45g; Sodium 837mg; Carbs 8.33g; Fiber 1.6g; Sugar 3.15g; Protein 26.52g

# Spicy Gingered Swordfish with Mango

Prep Time: 10 minutes | Cook Time: 35 minutes | Servings: 4

## Ingredients:

1 cup unsweetened coconut milk
½ cup chopped fresh ginger root
½ cup chopped red onion
1 teaspoon chili powder

Salt to taste
1 mango - peeled, seeded, and cubed
1 pound fresh swordfish, cut into chunks

## Instructions:

1. Combine salt, chili powder, red onion, ginger, and coconut milk in a medium-sized pan. Toss in mango and boil it. 2. Put swordfish pieces into the coconut extract mixture, lower the heat. Be careful to not crush the swordfish pieces, cook, tossing sometimes until the mixture is firm and the fish is flaky with a fork, about 25-30 minutes.
Per Serving: Calories 268; Fat 10.06g; Sodium 722mg; Carbs 19.31g; Fiber 2.1g; Sugar 15.42g; Protein 25.37g

# Steamed Salmon with Vegetables

## Prep Time: 10 minutes | Cook Time: 5 minutes | Servings: 4

**Ingredients:**

4 Salmon Fillets

2 tsp olive oil

1 large carrot, peeled and spiralized

2 large potatoes, peeled and spiralized

1 zucchini, peeled and spiralized

1 cup water

1 thyme sprig

¼ tsp pepper

¼ tsp salt

**Instructions:**

1. Pour the water into your Instant Pot and add the thyme sprig inside. 2. Arrange the noodles inside the steaming basket and top with the salmon. 3. Season with salt and pepper and drizzle with the oil. 4. Place the basket inside the Instant Pot. Close the lid and turn clockwise to seal. 5. Select the "STEAM" cooking mode. 6. Set the cooking time to 5 minutes. Cook on HIGH pressure. 7. When you hear the beep, press the "KEEP WARM/CANCEL" button. 8. Move the pressure handle from "Sealing" to "Venting" for a quick pressure release and open the lid carefully. 9. Remove the steaming basket from the Instant Pot gently, and serve the veggies and salmon. 10. Enjoy!

**Per Serving:** Calories 345; Fat 10.62g; Sodium 661mg; Carbs 34.46g; Fiber 4.7g; Sugar 2.44g; Protein 27.45g

# Salmon with Potatoes & Broccoli

## Prep Time: 3 minutes | Cook Time: 5 minutes | Servings: 1

**Ingredients:**

4-ounce salmon fillet

4 new potatoes

4 ounces broccoli florets

2 tsp olive oil

Salt and pepper, to taste

1½ cups water

**Instructions:**

1. Pour the water into your Instant Pot and lower the rack. 2. Season the potatoes with some salt and pepper and place them on top of the rack. Drizzle half of the oil over. 3. Close the lid and turn clockwise to seal. Select the "MANUAL" cooking mode and then the cooking time to 2 minutes. Cook on HIGH pressure. 4. When the timer goes off, press "KEEP WARM/CANCEL" to turn the Instant Pot off. 5. Move the handle to "Venting" to release the pressure quickly before opening the lid. 6. Season the broccoli and salmon with salt and pepper, as well. 7. Arrange the broccoli on top of the potatoes and top with the salmon fillet. 8. Drizzle them with the remaining olive oil. 9. Close and seal the lid again and cook on "MANUAL" for 3 more minutes. 10. Again, do a quick pressure release. 11. Serve and enjoy!

**Per Serving:** Calories 392; Fat 19.19g; Sodium 1594mg; Carbs 24.7g; Fiber 14.1g; Sugar 5.61g; Protein 37.87g

# Roasted Salmon with Tomatoes

## Prep Time: 20 minutes | Cook Time: 35 minutes | Servings: 4

### Ingredients:

3 pounds fresh or frozen salmon fillet(s), skinned if desired

Nonstick cooking spray

4 cups grape tomatoes

½ cup thinly sliced shallots

6 cloves garlic, minced

2 tablespoons snipped fresh oregano or 1½ teaspoons dried oregano, crushed

1 tablespoon olive oil

½ teaspoon salt

½ teaspoon ground black pepper

### Instructions:

1. Unfreeze fish if frozen. Wash the salmon and dab with paper towels to dry. Heat the oven to 400°F. 2. Lightly spray a 3-qt. baking tray with nonstick cooking spray. In the baking tray, put garlic, oregano, olive oil, ¼ tsp. salt, and ¼ tsp. pepper, tomatoes and shallots. Mix to coat the salmon. 3. Roast without cover for 15 minutes. Place salmon above the tomato-shallot mixture with the skin side facing down. Drizzle with the remaining ¼ tsp. pepper and ¼ tsp. salt. Roast without cover for 15 to 18 minutes until salmon flakes easily shreds when inserted with a fork. Use 2 big pancake flippers to transfer the salmon to a cutting board. 4. Set aside ⅔ cooked salmon for another meal. 5. If desired, use the flippers to remove the salmon meat from the skin and transfer into a big platter; put away the skin. Serve the tomato-shallot mixture on the remaining salmon.

Per Serving: Calories 889; Fat 31.31g; Sodium 1662mg; Carbs 106.83g; Fiber 6.9g; Sugar 25.51g; Protein 48.98g

# Chapter 6 Snack and Appetizer Recipes

# Grilled Mushrooms Stuffed with Onion Dip

## Prep Time: 10 minutes | Cook time: 20 minutes | Servings: 8

**Ingredients:**

1 pound cremini mushrooms caps

3 tablespoons olive oil

A pinch of cayenne pepper

For the dip:

1 cup coconut cream

½ cup mayonnaise

2 tablespoons coconut oil

1 yellow onion, chopped

A pinch of smoked paprika

Onion dip

¼ teaspoon white pepper

¼ teaspoon garlic powder

2 tablespoons green onions chopped

**Instructions:**

1. Heat up a pan with 2 tablespoons coconut oil over medium heat, add onion, garlic powder and white pepper, stir, cook for 10 minutes, take off heat and leave aside to cool down. 2. In a bowl, mix mayo with coconut cream, green onions and caramelized onions, stir well and keep in the fridge for now. 3. Season mushroom caps with a pinch of cayenne pepper and paprika and drizzle the olive oil over them. 4. Rub them, place on preheated grill over medium high heat and cook them for 5 minutes on each side. 5. Arrange them on a platter, stuff them with the onion dip and serve. 6. Enjoy!

**Per Serving:** Calories 413; Fat 25.44g; Sodium 127mg; Carbs 48.23g; Fiber 8g; Sugar 2.82g; Protein 7.86g

# Garlicky Chicken Skewers

## Prep Time: 3 hours | Cook time: 15 minutes | Servings: 4

**Ingredients:**

2 tablespoons parsley, chopped

4 chicken breasts, cubed

¾ cup garlic powder

Black pepper to taste

**Instructions:**

1. In a bowl, mix chicken with garlic powder, black pepper, and parsley, stir well, cover and keep in the fridge for 3 hours. 2. Arrange chicken pieces on skewers, place them all on preheated grill and cook for 15 minutes, flipping once. 3. Arrange skewers on a platter and serve as an appetizer. 4. Enjoy!

**Per Serving:** Calories 600; Fat 27.07g; Sodium 202mg; Carbs 22.35g; Fiber 2.9g; Sugar 1.3g; Protein 65.56g

# Crispy Kale Chips

## Prep Time: 10 minutes | Cook time: 20 minutes | Servings: 6

**Ingredients:**

1 tablespoon avocado oil

1 bunch kale, leaves separated

A pinch of sea salt

Black pepper to taste

**Instructions:**

1. Pat dry kale leaves, arrange them on a lined baking sheet, drizzle the oil, sprinkle a pinch of sea salt and black pepper to taste, place in the oven at 275°F and bake for 20 minutes. 2. Serve the chips cold. 3. Enjoy!

**Per Serving:** Calories 42; Fat 2.7g; Sodium 402mg; Carbs 4g; Fiber 1.5g; Sugar 1.24g; Protein 1.77g

# Rosemary Crackers

## Prep Time: 10 minutes | Cook time: 14 minutes | Servings: 40

**Ingredients:**

¼ cup coconut flour

1 cup almond flour

½ cup sesame seeds, toasted and ground

2 tablespoons tapioca flour

A pinch of sea salt

Black pepper to taste

1 teaspoon onion powder

1 teaspoon rosemary, chopped

½ teaspoon thyme, chopped

2 eggs

3 tablespoons olive oil

**Instructions:**

1. In a bowl, mix sesame seeds with coconut flour, almond flour, tapioca flour, salt, pepper, rosemary, thyme and onion powder and stir well. 2. In another bowl, whisk eggs with the oil and stir well. 3. Add this to flour mix and knead until you obtain a dough. 4. Shape a disk out of this dough, flatten well and cut 40 crackers out of it. 5. Arrange them all on a lined baking sheet, place in the oven at 375°F and bake for 14 minutes. 6. Leave your crackers to cool down and serve them as a snack. 7. Enjoy!

**Per Serving:** Calories 27; Fat 2.28g; Sodium 249mg; Carbs 1.11g; Fiber 0.3g; Sugar 0.16g; Protein 0.77g

# Coconut Sesame Seed Crackers

## Prep Time: 10 minutes | Cook time: 3 hours | Servings: 40

**Ingredients:**

½ cup chia seeds

1 cup flaxseed, ground

½ cup pumpkin seeds

⅓ cup sesame seeds

A pinch of sea salt

1 and ¼ cups water

½ teaspoon garlic powder

1 teaspoon thyme, dried

1 teaspoon basil, dried

**Instructions:**

1. Put pumpkin seeds in your food processor, pulse well and transfer them to a bowl. 2. Add flaxseed, sesame seeds, chia, salt, water, garlic powder, thyme and basil and stir well until they combine. 3. Spread this on a lined baking sheet, press well, cuts into 40 pieces, place in the oven at 200°F and bake for 3 hours. 4. Leave your crackers to cool down before serving them as a snack. 5. Enjoy!

**Per Serving:** Calories 44; Fat 3.56g; Sodium 122mg; Carbs 2.04g; Fiber 1.7g; Sugar 0.1g; Protein 1.64g

# Chocolate Coconut Bars

## Prep Time: 30 minutes | Cook time: 0 minutes | Servings: 10

**Ingredients:**

1 teaspoon vanilla extract

1 cup coconut flakes, unsweetened

2 cups cashews

1 and ¼ cups figs, dried

A pinch of sea salt

⅓ cup cocoa butter

¾ cup cocoa powder

1 tablespoon cocoa powder

**Instructions:**

1. In your food processor, mix figs with vanilla, cashews, a pinch of salt, cocoa powder and coconut and blend them well. 2. Transfer this into a baking dish and press well. 3. Put cocoa powder and cocoa butter in a heatproof bowl, place in your microwave for 3 minutes until it melts. 4. Pour this over coconut mix, spread well, place in your freezer for 20 minutes, cut into bars and serve as a snack. 5. Enjoy!

**Per Serving:** Calories 397; Fat 29.4g; Sodium 778mg; Carbs 31.75g; Fiber 5.9g; Sugar 13.13g; Protein 10.35g

# Roasted Almonds with Herbs

## Prep Time: 10 minutes | Cook time: 16 minutes | Servings: 4

**Ingredients:**

16 ounces almonds

Black pepper to taste

A pinch of sea salt

1 teaspoon sage, dried

½ teaspoon smoked paprika

1 tablespoon rosemary, chopped

1 tablespoon garlic powder

**Instructions:**

1. Spread the almonds on a lined baking sheet, add all the other ingredients, toss, place in the oven at 300°F and roast for 8 minutes. 2. Flip nuts and bake them for 8 minutes more. 3. Divide into bowls and serve as a snack. 4. Enjoy!

**Per Serving:** Calories 671; Fat 56.75g; Sodium 585mg; Carbs 27.62g; Fiber 14.8g; Sugar 5.6g; Protein 24.69g

# Chestnuts Apricot Bites

## Prep Time: 2 hours | Cook time: 40 minutes | Servings: 4

**Ingredients:**

10 apricots, dried

10 turkey fillet strips, cooked, cut in halves

10 ounces chestnuts, shelled, peeled, cooked

2 teaspoons lemongrass, chopped

4 tablespoons garlic, minced

½ cup coconut aminos

**Instructions:**

1. Cut an "X" shape into the flat side of each chestnut. Place the chestnuts in a microwave and bake for 5 minutes on max, then peel. Wrap a chestnut and an apricot in turkey strip and secure with a toothpick. 2. Repeat this with the rest of the ingredients. 3. Heat up a pan over medium-low heat, add garlic, stir and sauté it for 20 minutes. 4. Transfer garlic to a bowl, cool down, add lemongrass, coconut aminos and the apricot bites, cover and leave them aside for 2 hours. 5. Spread apricot bites on a lined baking sheet, place in the oven at 350°F and bake for 20 minutes. 6. Arrange them on a platter and serve as an appetizer. 7. Enjoy!

**Per Serving:** Calories 313; Fat 5.68g; Sodium 367mg; Carbs 42.65g; Fiber 7g; Sugar 6.24g; Protein 22.69g

# Turkey Stuffed Mushroom

**Prep Time: 10 minutes | Cook time: 30 minutes | Servings: 4**

**Ingredients:**

1 pound turkey meat, chopped

1 pound big white mushroom caps, stems separated and chopped

3 tablespoons coconut oil

1 yellow onion, chopped

A pinch of black pepper

**Instructions:**

1. Heat up a pan with 2 tablespoons oil over medium heat, add mushrooms stems, stir and cook them for 3 minutes. 2. Add the rest of the oil, onion and a pinch of black pepper, stir and cook for 7 minutes. 3. Transfer this mix to a bowl, add turkey meat and stir well. 4. Stuff mushrooms with this mix, place them on a lined baking sheet and bake in the oven at 400°F for 30 minutes. 5. Arrange mushrooms on a platter and serve them. 6. Enjoy!

Per Serving: Calories 348; Fat 19.59g; Sodium 81mg; Carbs 8.77g; Fiber 3g; Sugar 4.18g; Protein 34.94g

# Spicy Mushroom and Broccoli Skewers

**Prep Time: 20 minutes | Cook time: 10 minutes | Servings: 4**

**Ingredients:**

10 mushroom caps

½ teaspoon chili powder

1 cup broccoli florets

1 teaspoon garam masala

1 teaspoon ginger and garlic paste

½ teaspoon turmeric powder

A drizzle of olive oil

A pinch of sea salt

Black pepper to taste

**Instructions:**

1. In a bowl, mix chili powder, garam masala, ginger paste, turmeric, salt, pepper and oil and stir. 2. Add mushroom caps and broccoli florets, toss to coat well and keep in the fridge for 20 minutes. 3. Arrange these on skewers, place them on preheated grill over medium-high heat, cook for 5 minutes on each side and transfer to a platter. 4. Serve them as an appetizer. 5. Enjoy!

Per Serving: Calories 22; Fat 0.6g; Sodium 120mg; Carbs 3.41g; Fiber 1.1g; Sugar 1.57g; Protein 2.05g

# Cauliflower and Turkey Bites

## Prep Time: 10 minutes | Cook time: 30 minutes | Servings: 6

**Ingredients:**

20 ounces ground turkey

2 eggs, whisked

1 cup cauliflower, riced

1 and ½ tablespoon coconut oil

½ teaspoon baking soda

1 teaspoon apple cider vinegar

¼ cup coconut flour

1 teaspoon red pepper sauce

A pinch of sea salt

¼ teaspoon smoked paprika

½ teaspoon mustard powder

A pinch of chili powder

2 teaspoons jalapenos, chopped

**Instructions:**

1. In a bowl, mix the cauliflower rice with the coconut flour, eggs, oil, red pepper sauce, mustard, salt, chili powder, paprika and jalapenos and stir. 2. Add the baking soda and the vinegar and stir well again. 3. Place 12 spoonfuls of this mix on a lined baking sheet, put 1 tsp of turkey mince on each cauliflower circle, and top with other 12 spoonfuls of cauliflower mix. 4. Seal edges, place in the oven at 400°F and bake for 30 minutes. 5. Arrange on a platter and serve them. 6. Enjoy!

**Per Serving:** Calories 527; Fat 47.64g; Sodium 603mg; Carbs 1.91g; Fiber 0.7g; Sugar 0.9g; Protein 21.48g

# Avocado& Cucumber on Watermelon Circles

## Prep Time: 10 minutes | Cook time: 0 minutes | Servings: 20

**Ingredients:**

4 watermelon slices

1 avocado, peeled, pitted and chopped

½ cup cucumber, chopped

¼ cup red onion, chopped

1 teaspoon coconut aminos

1 teaspoon lime juice

**Instructions:**

1. Cut 20 circles of watermelon using a cookie cutter. 2. In a bowl, mix onion with avocado, aminos, cucumber and lime juice and stir well. 3. Divide this into watermelon circles, place them on a platter and serve. 4. Enjoy!

**Per Serving:** Calories 18; Fat 1.49g; Sodium 1mg; Carbs 1.19g; Fiber 0.7g; Sugar 0.32g; Protein 0.25g

# Bacon-Cucumber Rolls

## Prep Time: 10 minutes | Cook time: 0 minutes | Servings: 3

**Ingredients:**

1 cucumber, very thinly sliced

6 ham slices

1 jalapeno, chopped

3 teaspoons mayonnaise

1 teaspoon dill, chopped

6 green onions, chopped

**Instructions:**

1. Arrange ham slices on a working surface. 2. In a bowl, mix mayo with jalapeno, green onions and dill and stir well. 3. Spread some of this mix over 1 ham slice, add a cucumber slice at the end, roll cucumber around ham and secure with a toothpick. 4. Repeat with the remaining ingredients and serve as an appetizer. 5. Enjoy!

Per Serving: Calories 161; Fat 3.51g; Sodium 638mg; Carbs 22.97g; Fiber 4.4g; Sugar 10.49g; Protein 10.96g

# Turkey & Tomato Stuffed Zucchini Rolls

## Prep Time: 10 minutes | Cook time: 5 minutes | Servings: 4

**Ingredients:**

3 zucchinis, thinly sliced lengthwise

10 ounces turkey meat, cooked, sliced into thin strips

½ cup sun-dried tomatoes, drained and chopped

4 tablespoons raspberry vinegar

½ cup basil, chopped

A pinch of sea salt

Black pepper to taste

**Instructions:**

1. Place zucchini slices in a bowl, sprinkle a pinch of sea salt and vinegar over them and leave aside for 10 minutes. 2. Drain well and season with black pepper to taste. 3. Divide turkey slices, chopped sun dried tomatoes and basil over zucchini ones, roll each and secure with a toothpick and arrange them on a lined baking sheet. 4. Place in the oven at 400°F for 5 minutes, then arrange them on a platter and serve as an appetizer. 5. Enjoy!

Per Serving: Calories 149; Fat 4.33g; Sodium 636mg; Carbs 5.3g; Fiber 1.1g; Sugar 3.18g; Protein 21.52g

# Simple Cabbage Chips

## Prep Time: 10 minutes | Cook time: 2 hours | Servings: 8

**Ingredients:**

½ red cabbage head, leaves separated and halved

½ green cabbage head, leaves separated and halved

A drizzle of olive oil

Black pepper to taste

A pinch of sea salt

**Instructions:**

1. Spread cabbage leaves on a lined baking sheet, place in the oven at 200°F and bake for 2 hours. 2. Drizzle the oil over them, sprinkle salt and black pepper, rub well, transfer to a bowl and serve as a snack. 3. Enjoy!

**Per Serving:** Calories 31; Fat 0.87g; Sodium 325mg; Carbs 5.76g; Fiber 1.6g; Sugar 3g; Protein 1.13g

# Bacon-Wrapped Enoki Mushrooms

## Prep Time: 15 minutes | Cook Time: 12 minutes | Servings: 4

**Ingredients:**

1 pound enoki mushrooms;

6 slices bacon;

½ lemon;

**Instructions:**

1. Place 12 toothpicks in water to soak. 2. Trim the root of the mushrooms. Divide little clumps of mushrooms into 12 roughly equal bunches. 3. Cut your bacon slices in two. 4. Wrap a bacon slice around each bunch of enoki mushrooms. 5. Tuck any stray stems in there. Take one of the soaked toothpicks to skewer the bacon in place. Preheat the broiler. 6. Oil it and lay enoki bundles on it. Grill for 10-12 minutes turning carefully until the bacon is crisp and the enoki are brown. 7. Remove enoki from the broiler place them to a cutting board. 8. Cut each bundle in two. 9. Cut your half lemon into thin wedges, add one to each plate, and then serve.

**Per Serving:** Calories 496; Fat 16.45g; Sodium 198mg; Carbs 86.21g; Fiber 13.1g; Sugar 2.98g; Protein 15.77g

# Spicy Sweet Potatoes Chips

Prep Time: 10 minutes | Cook Time: 40 minutes | Servings: 4

**Ingredients:**

4 sweet potatoes; peeled and thinly sliced

2 tsp. nutmeg

2 tbsp. coconut oil; melted

Cayenne pepper to the taste

**Instructions:**

1. In a bowl; mix sweet potato slices with nutmeg, cayenne and oil and toss to coat really well. 2. Spread these on a lined baking sheet, place in the oven at 350°F and bake for 25 minutes. 3. Take potatoes out of the oven, flip them, put them back into the oven and bake for 15 minutes more. Serve as a tasty Paleo side dish!

Per Serving: Calories 181; Fat 7.29g; Sodium 72mg; Carbs 27.26g; Fiber 4.3g; Sugar 6.04g; Protein 2.33g

# Homemade Mexican Mole

Prep Time: 15 minutes | Cook Time: 20 minutes | Servings:20

**Ingredients:**

20 roma (plum) tomatoes

8 fresh jalapeno peppers

¼ cup crushed walnuts

⅓ cup sesame seeds

¼ cup raisins

3 ounces bittersweet chocolate, melted

2 tablespoons minced garlic

1 quart vegetable stock

**Instructions:**

1. Set up the broiler for preheating. On a baking sheet, place jalapeno peppers and tomatoes, then broil until they begins to scorch on all sides while turning one time, for 5 minutes. Take away from the heat, then put peppers into a bowl and use plastic wrap to cover tightly for 15 minutes, until cooled. Slip the skins off the peppers and slit peppers open to get rid of the seeds. 2. Blend together garlic, chocolate, raisins, sesame seeds, walnuts, peppers and tomatoes in a food processor or blender. 3. Spray a skillet with cooking spray and heat on moderately high heat. Cook and stir the blended mixture in the skillet until heated through. 4. Turn the mixture back to blender, then blend in sufficient vegetable stock to create a lightly thick sauce. Let the mixture cool and store in the fridge until using.

Per Serving: Calories 64; Fat 2.59g; Sodium 39mg; Carbs 9.36g; Fiber 2.3g; Sugar 5.8g; Protein 2.15g

# Foil Wrapped Potatoes and Green Beans

## Prep Time: 15 minutes | Cook Time: 30 minutes | Servings: 10

**Ingredients:**

2½ pounds new potatoes, thinly sliced

1 large sweet potato, thinly sliced

2 Vidalia onions, sliced ¼ inch thick

½ pound fresh green beans, cut into 1 inch pieces

1 sprig fresh rosemary

1 sprig fresh thyme

2 tablespoons olive oil

salt and pepper to taste

¼ cup olive oil

**Instructions:**

1. Preheat a grill to high heat. 2. Mix thyme, rosemary, green beans. Vidalia onions, sweet potato and new potatoes in a big bowl. Mix pepper, salt and 2 tbsp. olive oil in to coat. 3. Create desired number of foil packets with 2-3 foil layers. Liberally brush leftover olive oil the inside surfaces of packets. Distribute veggie mixture among packets evenly. Tightly seal. 4. On preheated grill, put packets. Cook, turning once, for 30 minutes or till potatoes are tender.

**Per Serving:** Calories 183; Fat 8.36g; Sodium 14mg; Carbs 25.21g; Fiber 3.7g; Sugar 2.53g; Protein 3.04g

# Grilled Garlicky Yellow Squash

## Prep Time: 10 minutes | Cook Time: 20 minutes | Servings: 4

**Ingredients:**

4 medium yellow squash

½ cup extra virgin olive oil

2 cloves garlic, crushed

salt and pepper to taste

**Instructions:**

1. Preheat a grill to medium heat. 2. Horizontally, cut squash to ¼-in. – ½-in. thick slices to get long strips that won't fall through grill. 3. In a small pan, heat olive oil; add garlic cloves. Cook on medium heat till garlic is fragrant and starts to sizzle. Brush garlic oil on squash slices. Season with pepper and salt. 4. Grill squash slices till they reach desired tenderness or for 5-10 minutes per side. Brush with extra garlic oil. Occasionally turning to avoid burning or sticking.

**Per Serving:** Calories 143; Fat 11.98g; Sodium 237mg; Carbs 8.13g; Fiber 2.4g; Sugar 4.9g; Protein 2.8g

# Stir-Fry Eggplant

## Prep Time: 10 minutes | Cook time: 20 minutes | Servings: 4

**Ingredients:**

4 cups eggplant, sliced

½ tsp ground ginger

½ tsp red pepper flakes

5 tbsp tamari sauce

1 tbsp olive oil

1 bell pepper, sliced

3 garlic cloves, minced

1 onion, chopped

**Instructions:**

1. Heat oil in a pan over medium-high heat. 2. Add onion and garlic and sauté for 6-8 minutes. 3. Turn heat to medium and add eggplant and bell pepper. 4. Stir well and cook for few minutes. 5. Add red pepper flakes, ginger, and tamari and stir well. 6. Cook for 12 minutes. Stir occasionally. 7. Serve and enjoy.

**Per Serving:** Calories 77; Fat 3.63g; Sodium 163mg; Carbs 10.9g; Fiber 3.6g; Sugar 5.57g; Protein 1.84g

# Grilled Lemony Romaine Lettuce

## Prep Time: 10 minutes | Cook Time: 5 minutes | Servings: 4

**Ingredients:**

1 tablespoon olive oil

1 head romaine lettuce, cut in half lengthwise

1 tablespoon steak seasoning

1 lemon, juiced

**Instructions:**

1. Preheat the grill to medium heat. Oil the grate lightly. Drizzle olive oil on romaine lettuce. Season using steak seasoning. 2. On the preheated grill, put the lettuce, cut side down. Cook for 5 minutes till lettuce is charred and slightly wilted. Drizzle lemon juice and serve.

**Per Serving:** Calories 66; Fat 3.87g; Sodium 168mg; Carbs 7.22g; Fiber 3.6g; Sugar 2.4g; Protein 2.06g

# Chapter 7 Dessert Recipes

# Easy Chocolate Parfait

Prep Time: 2 hours | Cook time: 0 minutes | Servings: 4

## Ingredients:

2 tablespoons cocoa powder
1 cup almond milk
1 tablespoon chia seeds

A pinch of salt
½ teaspoon vanilla extract

## Instructions:

1. In a bowl, mix cocoa powder, almond milk, vanilla extract and chia seeds and stir well until they blend. 2. Transfer to a dessert glass, place in the fridge for 2 hours and then serve. 3. Enjoy!

Per Serving: Calories 63; Fat 3.5g; Sodium 221mg; Carbs 6.14g; Fiber 2.1g; Sugar 3.19g; Protein 3.03g

# Tropical Fruit with Coconut Cream

Prep Time: 20 minutes | Cook Time: 15 minutes | Servings: 4

## Ingredients:

1 banana
1 mango
½ pineapple
1 papaya
1 can coconut milk

1 cup coconut flakes
2 tablespoons sliced almonds
1 teaspoon almond/ vanilla extract
¼ teaspoon salt
¼ teaspoon dash cinnamon

## Instructions:

1. Place a can coconut milk in the fridge at least 3-4 hours beforehand. When starting cooking, put it in the freezer for 15 minutes. 2. Wash the banana, mango, pineapple and papaya, dry them with paper towels, dice them and divide among 4 bowls. 3. Pre-heat a pan over medium-high heat for 2 minutes. Put the coconut flakes on the pan and distribute them on the surface, stir for 3 minutes till they're ready. 4. Combine salt with cinnamon in a mold. Add them to the coconut flakes, stir and remove them from the pan to a plate to let them cool. 5. Heat a pan over medium-high heat again. Put the sliced almond on the pan, stir for 3-5 minutes, and place it on the plate. 6. Pour the cold coconut milk into the mixing bowl, add almond/vanilla extract. Whip it at the highest speed for 5-7 minutes till the milk is whipped to a creamy structure. 7. Add cooled coconut flakes, the sliced almond to fruit in the bowls, put the whipped coconut cream at the top.

Per Serving: Calories 264; Fat 7.01g; Sodium 266mg; Carbs 51.74g; Fiber 7.2g; Sugar 38.61g; Protein 2.98g

# Delicious Chestnut Cream

## Prep Time: 10 minutes | Cook time: 3 hours | Servings: 10

**Ingredients:**

4 tablespoons stevia

11 ounces water

1 and ½ pounds chestnuts, halved and peeled

**Instructions:**

1. In your Crockpot, mix stevia with water and chestnuts, stir, cover and cook on Low for 3 hours. Blend using your immersion blender, divide into small cups and serve. 2. Enjoy!

**Per Serving:** Calories 97; Fat 1.03g; Sodium 2mg; Carbs 26.66g; Fiber 3.7g; Sugar 0g; Protein 1.1g

# Rhubarb Strawberry Mousse

## Prep Time: 10 minutes | Cook time: 3 hours | Servings: 10

**Ingredients:**

1 cup water

2 pounds rhubarb, chopped

2 tablespoon stevia

⅓ pound strawberries, chopped

**Instructions:**

1. Put rhubarb, water, stevia and strawberries In your Crockpot, cover and cook on High for 3 hours. Divide between bowls and serve cold. 2. Enjoy!

**Per Serving:** Calories 110; Fat 0.09g; Sodium 2mg; Carbs 32.45g; Fiber 2.1g; Sugar 26.77g; Protein 0.45g

# Green Apple and Spinach Smoothie

## Prep Time: 10 minutes | Cook time: 0 minutes | Servings: 3

**Ingredients:**

1 big green apple, cored and cut into medium cubes

1 cup baby spinach

1 tablespoon pure maple syrup

A pinch of cardamom

½ teaspoon cinnamon

½ teaspoon vanilla extract

**Instructions:**

1. Put apple cubes in a food processor. 2. Add spinach, maple syrup, vanilla extract, cardamom and cinnamon and blend until you obtain a smooth cream. 3. Pour into 2 glasses and serve right away! 4. Enjoy!

**Per Serving:** Calories 56; Fat 0.2g; Sodium 10mg; Carbs 14.1g; Fiber 2.1g; Sugar 10.47g; Protein 0.54g

# Mixed Fruit Bowls

## Prep Time: 6 hours and 10 minutes | Cook time: 0 minutes | Servings: 6

**Ingredients:**

1 cup apples, chopped
1 cup pineapple, chopped
1 cup chickoo, chopped
1 cup melon, chopped
1 cup papaya, chopped

½ teaspoon vanilla powder
¾ cup cashews
Stevia to the taste
Some cold water

**Instructions:**

1. Put cashews in a bowl, add some water on top, leave aside for 6 hours, drain them and put them in a food processor. 2. Blend them well and add cold water to cover them. 3. Also add stevia and vanilla, blend some more and keep in the fridge for now. 4. In a bowl, arrange a layer of mixed apples with pineapples, melon, papaya and chickoo. 5. Add a layer of cold cashew paste, another layer of fruits, another one of cashew paste and to with a layer of fruits. 6. Serve right away!
**Per Serving:** Calories 311; Fat 20.08g; Sodium 117mg; Carbs 25.32g; Fiber 2.6g; Sugar 16.15g; Protein 11.23g

# Pecans Squash Pudding

## Prep Time: 10 minutes | Cook time: 4 hours | Servings: 8

**Ingredients:**

Cooking spray
2 tablespoons stevia
3 eggs
½ cup almond flour
½ teaspoon allspice, ground
½ teaspoon cinnamon powder

A pinch of nutmeg
½ teaspoon baking soda
⅔ cup ghee, melted
½ cup pecans, chopped
1 cup butternut squash, grated

**Instructions:**

1. In a bowl, mix stevia with eggs, almond flour, allspice, cinnamon, nutmeg, baking soda, melted ghee, pecans, squash, stir well, pour Into your Crockpot after you've greased it with cooking spray, cover and cook on Low for 4 hours. Leave pudding to cool down, slice and serve. 2. Enjoy!
**Per Serving:** Calories 103; Fat 8.32g; Sodium 118mg; Carbs 7.52g; Fiber 1.2g; Sugar 0.9g; Protein 4.16g

# Vanilla Hemp Hearts

## Prep Time: 10 minutes | Cook time: 1 hour and 30 minutes | Servings: 4

**Ingredients:**

1 cup coconut milk

1 cup hemp hearts

2 and ½ cups water

½ tablespoon stevia

1 teaspoon espresso powder

2 teaspoons vanilla extract

**Instructions:**

1. In your Crockpot, mix hemp with water, stevia, milk and espresso powder, stir, cover and cook on High for 1 hour and 30 minutes Add vanilla extract, stir, divide between bowls and serve cold 2. Enjoy!

**Per Serving:** Calories 56; Fat 2.23g; Sodium 185mg; Carbs 6.09g; Fiber 1g; Sugar 3.39g; Protein 2.91g

# Mulberry and Dates Cupcakes

## Prep Time: 1 hour and 10 minutes | Cook time: 0 minutes | Servings: 6

**Ingredients:**

16 ounces mulberries, dried

1 teaspoon cinnamon, ground

16 ounces dates, pitted and chopped

3 ounces almond butter

3 ounces raw beet juice powder

3 ounces spirulina powder

8 ounces coconut water

1 and ½ cups raw cashews

**Instructions:**

1. In a food processor, mix mulberries with dates, cinnamon and butter and blend well. Scoop this mix into a cupcake pan and leave aside. 2. Clean the food processor, mix spirulina powder with half of the cashews and half of the coconut water, blend well. Transfer to a bowl and leave aside. 3. Clean the blender again, add beet powder with the rest of the cashews and the coconut water and pulse well. 4. Decorate half of the cupcakes with the beets frosting and the other half with the spirulina powder one. 5. Keep cupcakes in the fridge for 1 hour and serve them. 6. Enjoy!

**Per Serving:** Calories 625; Fat 34.88g; Sodium 291mg; Carbs 80.52g; Fiber 9.7g; Sugar 59.9g; Protein 9.59g

# Cherry, Chocolate and Coconut Bark

## Prep Time: 30 minutes | Cook Time: 0 minutes | Servings: 3-5

**Ingredients:**

240ml coconut oil

2 tablespoons dried cherries

2 tablespoons coconut flakes

1 tablespoon chocolate chips

½ teaspoon vanilla extract

½ teaspoon almond extract

¼ vanilla bean

**Instructions:**

1. Let coconut oil soften in room temperature, put into the bowl. 2. Add dried cherries, chocolate chips, vanilla and almond extracts and vanilla bean to the coconut oil and mix it thoroughly. 3. Cover the plate with parchment paper, distribute the mixture over it. 4. Strew the mixture with coconut flakes and put it in the freezer for 20-30 minutes till it hardens. 5. Break the solid bark into pieces and serve

**Per Serving:** Calories 562; Fat 60.94g; Sodium 15mg; Carbs 8.52g; Fiber 0.6g; Sugar 6.47g; Protein 0.38g

# Tasty Banana Pancakes

## Prep Time: 10 minutes | Cook Time: 5 minutes | Servings: 10-12

**Ingredients:**

4 ripe bananas

2-3 eggs

4 tablespoons almond butter

1 tablespoons coconut oil

**Instructions:**

1. Wash the bananas, dry them, take off the skin, mash the bananas in a bowl. 2. Break the eggs into the bowl with mashed bananas, add almond butter, mix thoroughly. 3. Pre-heat a non-stick pan over the medium heat for 2 minutes, add coconut oil. 4. Pour some mixture on the pan, distribute to make a pancake. Cook it for 1-2 minutes, toss it and cook till it's ready. Repeat with the rest of the mixture. 5. Put the pancakes on the plates.

**Per Serving:** Calories 115; Fat 7.76g; Sodium 57mg; Carbs 10.03g; Fiber 1.1g; Sugar 5.4g; Protein 2.55g

# Special Vanilla Apple Cake

**Prep Time: 15 minutes | Cook time: 2 hours and 20 minutes | Servings: 6**

**Ingredients:**

3 cups apples, cored and cubed

⅓ cup swerve

1 tablespoon vanilla

2 eggs

1 tablespoon pumpkin pie spice

2 cups almond flour

1 tablespoon baking powder

1 tablespoon ghee, melted

**Instructions:**

1. In your Crockpot, mix apples with swerve, vanilla, eggs, apple pie spice, almond flour, baking powder and ghee, cover and cook on High for 2 hours and 20 minutes. Leave the special cake to cool down, slice and serve. 2. Enjoy!

**Per Serving:** Calories 126; Fat 4.11g; Sodium 36mg; Carbs 18.35g; Fiber 1.7g; Sugar 14.48g; Protein 3.4g

# Mango and Passion Fruit Sorbet

**Prep Time: 15 minutes | Cook Time: 0 minutes | Servings: 4-6**

**Ingredients:**

2 passion fruit

1-2 mangos

1 egg

1 tablespoon honey

**Instructions:**

1. Wash the fruit and dry them well with paper towels. 2. Peel off and dice mango, dice passion fruit. 3. Separate egg white from yolk, beat the egg white up to stiff peaks. 4. Put diced mango, passion fruit and honey in the electrical blender and blend it till they have homogenous creamy structure. 5. Add the mixture to beaten egg white, mix thoroughly. 6. Pour the mixture into container and place it in the refrigerator for at least 6 hours. 7. Cut into pieces when serving.

**Per Serving:** Calories 106; Fat 2.36g; Sodium 24mg; Carbs 20.45g; Fiber 2.4g; Sugar 18.15g; Protein 2.79g

# Conclusion

After completing the 30-Day Whole Foods Challenge, it's time to reflect on the experience. What was the most challenging part of the challenge? What did you learn about yourself? What are your thoughts on 30-Day Whole Foods now? The most challenging part of the challenge for me was giving up processed foods. I'm so used to eating packaged snacks and meals that it was hard to let go of that convenience. I also had to get used to cooking more meals from scratch. I learned that I enjoy cooking and eating whole foods. I feel so much better when I'm eating healthy, homemade meals. I also realized that I don't need processed foods to be happy or satisfied. Overall, I'm really happy that I completed the challenge. I feel better physically and mentally, and I'm proud of myself for committing to eating healthier. If you're considering doing the challenge of 30-Day Whole Foods, I say go for it! It's worth it.

# Appendix 1 Measurement Conversion Chart

## VOLUME EQUIVALENTS (LIQUID)

| US STANDARD | US STANDARD (OUNCES) | METRIC (APPROXIMATE) |
|---|---|---|
| 2 tablespoons | 1 fl.oz | 30 mL |
| ¼ cup | 2 fl.oz | 60 mL |
| ½ cup | 4 fl.oz | 120 mL |
| 1 cup | 8 fl.oz | 240 mL |
| 1½ cup | 12 fl.oz | 355 mL |
| 2 cups or 1 pint | 16 fl.oz | 475 mL |
| 4 cups or 1 quart | 32 fl.oz | 1 L |
| 1 gallon | 128 fl.oz | 4 L |

## VOLUME EQUIVALENTS (DRY)

| US STANDARD | METRIC (APPROXIMATE) |
|---|---|
| ⅛ teaspoon | 0.5 mL |
| ¼ teaspoon | 1 mL |
| ½ teaspoon | 2 mL |
| ¾ teaspoon | 4 mL |
| 1 teaspoon | 5 mL |
| 1 tablespoon | 15 mL |
| ¼ cup | 59 mL |
| ½ cup | 118 mL |
| ¾ cup | 177 mL |
| 1 cup | 235 mL |
| 2 cups | 475 mL |
| 3 cups | 700 mL |
| 4 cups | 1 L |

## TEMPERATURES EQUIVALENTS

| FAHRENHEIT(F) | CELSIUS(C) (APPROXIMATE) |
|---|---|
| 225 °F | 107 °C |
| 250 °F | 120 °C |
| 275 °F | 135 °C |
| 300 °F | 150 °C |
| 325 °F | 160 °C |
| 350 °F | 180 °C |
| 375 °F | 190 °C |
| 400 °F | 205 °C |
| 425 °F | 220 °C |
| 450 °F | 235 °C |
| 475 °F | 245 °C |
| 500 °F | 260 °C |

## WEIGHT EQUIVALENTS

| US STANDARD | METRIC (APPROXINATE) |
|---|---|
| 1 ounce | 28 g |
| 2 ounces | 57 g |
| 5 ounces | 142 g |
| 10 ounces | 284 g |
| 15 ounces | 425 g |
| 16 ounces (1 pound) | 455 g |
| 1.5pounds | 680 g |
| 2pounds | 907 g |

# Appendix 2 Recipes Index

Made in the USA
Las Vegas, NV
24 November 2023

81379542R00060